A Wales Millennium Centre Production

ES&FLO

By **Jennifer Lunn**

First performed at Wales Millennium Centre,
Cardiff on 28 April 2023

Winner of The Popcorn Writing Award 2020 and the
Nancy Dean Lesbian Playwriting Award 2022

CANOLFAN MILENIWM CYMRU
WALES MILLENNIUM CENTRE

Director **Susie McKenna**
Set & Costume Designer **Libby Watson**
Lighting Designer **Simisola Majekodunmi**
Sound Designer & Composer **Tic Ashfield**
Casting Director **Nadine Rennie CDG**
Associate Director **Alice Eklund**
Movement Director **Dollie Henry MBE**
Intimacy Co-ordinator **Ingrid Mackinnon**

Producer **Pádraig Cusack**

PERFORMED BY

Doreene Blackstock
Liz Crowther
Reesie Dupe (Cardiff)
Renée Hart (London)
Michelle McTernan
Chioma Nduka (London)
Adrianna Pavlovska
Mirella Siciliano (Cardiff)

PRODUCTION TEAM

Production Manager **Sarah Hemsley-Cole** *for SC Productions Ltd*
Company Stage Manager **Antonia Collins**
Deputy Stage Manager **Amy Hales**
Assistant Stage Manager **Zoe Wale**
Projection Designer **Phil Bearman**
Costumer Supervisor **Amy Barrett**
Lighting Programmer **Grace Priest**
Sound Engineer **Josh Bowles**
Production Staff for WMC **Ed Wilson**, **Eugene Capper**
Wardrobe Maintenance **Deryn Tudor**

Artwork by Wales Millennium Centre with photography by Kirsten McTernan

MEET THE WRITER

Jennifer Lunn
Playwright

Training: Rose Bruford College and Stephen. F. Austin State University, Texas.

Writing Credits: *Terroir* (RWCMD/ Sherman Theatre), *Stop The Drop* (Curtain Up – Theatr Clwyd), *Disorder – The Real Name Cannot Be Published* (RWCMD).

Jennifer won the Popcorn New Writing Award in 2020 and was the 2022 recipient of the American prize for new writing, the Nancy Dean Lesbian Playwriting Award, both for *Es & Flo*. It was also shortlisted for the Verity Bargate Award and longlisted for the Bruntwood Prize. Her second play *Core* was shortlisted for the Women's Prize for Playwriting in 2021 and the Papatango Prize in 2022. A filmed reading of *Core* is available via The Playwrights Laboratory.

Jennifer is also a producer and director having worked with National Theatre, Theatr Clwyd, Sherman Theatre, Wales Millennium Centre, Spare Tyre, Grand Ambition, Ellie Keel Productions, Leeway Productions and Dirty Protest.

MEET THE CAST

Doreene Blackstock
Flo

Theatre includes: *FOXES* (Seven Dials Playhouse); *The Key Workers Cycle* (Almeida Theatre); *FOXES* (Theatre503 & Theatre Peckham); *#846LIVE* (Theatre Royal, Stratford East); *Unknown Rivers* (Hampstead Theatre); *Equus* (Trafalgar Studios); *Noughts and Crosses* (Pilot Theatre Tour); *Bullet Hole, Distance* (Park Theatre); *Much Ado About Nothing* (The Globe); *Roundelay* (Southwark Playhouse); *Cymbeline, Hamlet, Noughts & Crosses* (RSC); *Antigone, Loneliness of the Long Distance Runner* (Pilot Theatre Company); *Holloway Jones* (Synergy Theatre Project); *The Container* (Young Vic Theatre); *Any Which Way* (Only Connect Theatre); *One Under, The Gift* (Tricycle Theatre); *25/7* (Talking Birds Theatre Company); *Document Given To Me By a Young Lady from Rwanda* (Ice & Fire Theatre Company); *The Carver Chair* (Contact Theatre); *Leave Taking, Girlie Talk* (Belgrade Studio); *Rosie & Jim's Big Adventure* (Ragdoll Theatre Company); *Leonora's Dance* (Black Theatre Co-operative).

TV and Film includes: *The Colour Room* (Sky); *Sex Education* (Netflix – Seasons 1, 2 & 3); *Doctors* (BBC); *Death in Paradise* (BBC); *The Child in Time* (Pinewood/BBC);

EastEnders (BBC); The Game (BBC); Silent Witness (BBC); Trinity (ITV); The Bill (Thames); Life Begins (ITV); Family Business (Tiger Aspect); Wire in the Blood (Coastal Productions); Medics (Granada); Casualty (BBC); Holby City (BBC); Judge John Deed (BBC); Gimme Gimme Gimme (BBC); Tom Jones (BBC); Common as Muck (BBC); Mm Hm; This Year's Love (Kismet Films).

Liz Crowther
Es

Training: Arts Educational, London and École Jacques Lecoq, Paris.

Theatre includes: A Midsummer Night's Dream (Regents Park Open Air); Visitors (Oldham Coliseum); The Wisdom Club (Bury St Edmunds); The Disappearing Act (Open Sky), A Passage to India (Simple8 and Park Theatre); Cardenio, The City Madam, Marat Sade, The White Devil, The Witch of Edmonton, The Roaring Girl and Song of Songs (RSC Stratford); Kite (Soho Theatre and the London Mime Festival); The Middlemarch Trilogy and 25 other plays (Orange Tree); Richard III as Richard (AFTLS tour of American universities and the Cockpit London); The Country Wife (Haymarket); Onassis (Novello); Ducktastic (West End); Cyrano de Bergerac (Royal Exchange); Romeo and Juliet (AFTLS, Globe and Rose Theatre); Abigail's Party (Hampstead Theatre tour); The Real Thing (UK tour); Communicating Doors (Stephen Joseph and

Chicago International Theatre Festival); Animal Farm and Four Short Becketts (National Theatre); Running Wild, Twelfth Night, The Merry Wives of Windsor and Oliver Twist (Regents Park).

Liz is very proud to be part of the Separate Doors Company which integrates trained actors with learning difficulties and she performed with them recently at Derby and Chichester Theatres. She also loves working for Scene and Heard, a fantastic child playwrighting , mentoring project working with the children of Somerstown.

Television includes: Vera – Christmas Special (BBC); The Following Events Are Based on a Pack of Lies (BBC/Sister Productions); Miss Scarlet and the Duke (BBC); The Chelsea Detective (BBC); Mansfield Park (BBC); Eastenders (BBC); Outnumbered (BBC); The Dumping Ground (BBC) and Holby City (BBC).

Reesie Dupe
Kasia
Cardiff performances

Training: Reesie has been a member of The Talent Shack in Cardiff since 2021 where along with friends is able to collaborate in writing plays, designing sets and of course putting on some very good plays!

Television: Casualty (BBC).

Music: Reesie is a keen drummer; she is currently the percussion for

Glamorgan Music School wind band and in the holidays, she loves to gig with Rock school.

Theatre: Reesie is thrilled to be making her stage début as Kasia in *Es & Flo*.

Renée Hart
Kasia
London performances

This is Renée's first time performing at the Kiln. Her recent début theatre performance was in the role of Little Hortense in *Small Island* at the National Theatre. After workshopping the role last year, Renée is very excited about being back on stage with the cast of *Es & Flo*.

Michelle McTernan
Catherine

Theatre includes: *MaryLand* (Sherman Theatre); *Revlon Girl* (Nearside Productions - Edinburgh Fringe, Park Theatre); *The Three Night Blitz* (Joio Productions/ Swansea Grand Theatre); *A Midsummer Night's Dream*, (Pontardawe Arts Centre); *Revlon Girl, Barren* (October Sixty Six Productions); *Bara Bread* (Theatr Gwalia); *Macbeth, The Merchant Of Venice, Buoy, Fall Out 84* (Pontardawe Arts Centre); *Granny Annie, Trivial Pursuits, Erogenous Zones, Roots And Wings, Family Planning, Kiss On The Bottom* (Grassroots Productions); *Flesh And Blood* (Sherman Theatre/ Hampstead Theatre); *The Oystercatchers* (Swansea Grand/Sherman Theatre); *Blue Remembered Hills* (Torch Theatre); *Under Milk Wood, Rosencrantz And Guildenstern Are Dead* (Clwyd Theatr Cymru/Tour); *Twelfth Night, Cymbeline, The Merchant Of Venice* (Ludlow Festival); *And* (Wales Theatre Company/Tour).

Television & Film includes: *The Crown* (Netflix); *Casualty* (BBC1); *The Lost Viking Sisters* (Tornado Productions); *Aetheled, Tree Bastards,* (Tornado Films/ Nowwherefast Productions); *The Healers* (Pooka Films); *Stella* (Tidy Productions, Sky1 HD); *Rain* (Tornado Films); *Caerdydd* (S4C); *Midnight* (Nowwhere Fast Productions); *Dr Terrible's House Of Horrible* (BBC); *Tales From Pleasure Beach* (BBC1); *Light In The City* (BBC Wales); *Very Annie Mary* (Dragon Pictures); *Bobinogs* (Cbeebies/BBC Wales/Worldwide).

Chioma Nduka
Kasia
London performances

Training: Deborah Day Theatre School.

Theatre: *Drifter Girl* (West End).

Chioma is delighted to be joining the cast of *Es & Flo* at Kiln Theatre in London.

Adrianna Pavlovska
Beata

Training: East15 Acting School

Theatre: *The Lower Depths* (Arcola Theatre); *White(Other)* (Pole Vault Theatre Company, The Warren, Brighton Fringe); *Burn* (Tristan Bates Theatre).

Television: *The Tower* (ITV).

Mirella Siciliano
Kasia
Cardiff performances

Training: Mirella lives in Cardiff and trains with Shelly Barrett's Talent Shack. Mirella also plays percussion, violin and piano, and recently started playing basketball.

Television: *Somewhere Boy* (Channel 4).

Film: *Jackdaw* (BAFTA Cymru nominated)

Theatre: Mirella is very proud to be joining the cast of *Es & Flo* in the role of Kasia.

MEET THE CREATIVE TEAM

Susie McKenna
Director

Susie has been an Actor, Writer and Director in Theatre, Film and Television for 40 years. She wrote and directed Hackney Empire's critically acclaimed pantomime for 22 years where she was also an Associate Director from 2005 and Creative Director from 2010 - 2017. From 2019 Susie was an Associate Director at Kiln Theatre for 2 and a half years.

Theatre: *Jungle Rumble* (Fortune Theatre); *NW Trilogy* (Kiln); *Blues In The Night* (Kiln – Olivier Award nominated); *The Silver Sword* (Belgrade Theatre Coventry/ National tour – Writer and Director); *Oranges and Elephants* (Hoxton Hall – OFFIE Nominated); *A Christmas Carol* (Arts Theatre); *Once On This Island* (Birmingham Rep/Nottingham Playhouse/ Hackney Empire); *Sit and Shiver, King, Abyssynia Praise Singer, Blues In The Night* (all Hackney Empire); *Ha Ha Hackney* (Sixty Years of British Comedy Festival); *Sophie Tucker's Once Night Stand* (Kings Head/Edinburgh Festival/ Hackney Empire); *A Midsummer Night Madness* (Harlem Festival NYC/Edinburgh Festival/Hackney Empire); *Macbeth* (Edinburgh

Festival); *Face Value* (Hackney Empire).

Television (as Producer): *Battles Axes* (Channel 4); *Journey Into Evil* (ABC/Channel 5).

Awards: Susie was the Hackney Empire Artist of the Year in 2000. She has been nominated twice for the Gilder/Coigney International Theatre Award with nominations for Best Director, Best Show and Best Script for Aladdin in 2018. In 2020 Susie won Best Director for her Windrush adaptation of *Dick Whittington* at the Great British Pantomime Awards 2020/21.

Libby Watson
Set & Costume Designer

Training: Bristol Old Vic Theatre School and Wimbledon School of Art (First Class BA Hons degree in Theatre Design)

Theatre: *Glitterball* (Watford Palace Thetre, Rifco Theatre); *The Fellowship* (Hampstead Theatre); *Tony! [The Tony Blair Rock Opera]* (Park Theatre London); *Bring It On: The Musical* (UK tour); *Toast by Nigel Slater* (West End & UK tour); *Being Mr Wickham* (Live stream & UK tour); *The Witchfinder's Sister* (Queens Theatre); *Dr Faustus* (Sam Wanamker Theatre); *Trolle, Helt Privat* (Kilden Theatre, Norway); *The Philanthropist* (Trafalgar Studios West End), *A Midsummer Night's Dream* directed by Sir Trevor Nunn, (New Wolsey Theatre);

Once (UK tour); *Daisy Pulls it Off* (Park Theatre); *Peter Pan* (Misi Producciones Bogota Columbia); *Fences* (West End, Theatre Royal Bath) *Single, One Man Two Guvnors, Guys and Dolls* (Wolsey Theatre); *Les Femmes Savantes, The Miser* (Belgrade Theatre); *Rudy's Rare Records* (Birmingham Rep, Hackney Empire); *Propoganda Swing* (Belgrade, Nottingham Playhouse); *Frankie and Johnny* (Chichester Festival); *History Boys* (UK tour); *Play Mas* (Orange Tree); *Feed the Beast, Hysteria* (Birmingham Rep); *Mustapha Matura's Three Sisters* (UK tour); *Gem of the Ocean, Blues for Mr Charlie, Radio Golf and The War Next Door* (Kiln Theatre); *One Monkey Don't Stop No Show* (Sheffield Crucible, UK tour); *Blonde Bombshells of 1943* (Hampstead Theatre, UK tour); *Blest Be The Tie, What's in the Cat* (Royal Court).

Libby designed the premiere of Katori Hall's *The Mountaintop* in the West End which was the winner of 2010 Olivier Award for Best Play.

Simisola Majekodunmi
Lighting Designer

Training: Royal Academy of Dramatic Arts (RADA), degree in Lighting Design

Theatre: *Sound of the Underground, Is God Is, Living Newspaper* (Royal Court); *Treason: The Musical in Concert* (Theatre Royal Dury Lane); *A Christmas Carole* (Palace

Theatre Southend); *Starcrossed* (Wilton's Music Hall); *Electric Rosary* (Royal Exchange Theatre); *A Christmas Carol* (Shakespeare North Playhouse); *Nine Night* (Leeds Playhouse); *Jungle Rumble* (Fortune Theatre); *Human Nurture* (Sheffield Theatres); *The Wiz* (Hope Mill Theatre); *Transformations* (New Public); *J'OUVERT* (Theatre503/ West End); *Driving Miss Daisy, Baby Box* (Theatre Royal, York); *Invisible Harmony* (Southbank); *Puck's Shadow* (Watford Palace).

Dance: *Traplord* (180 Studios); *The UK Drill Project* (Barbican); *Born to Exist* (Netherlands and UK tour); *AZARA - Just Another Day & Night* (The Place).

Tic Ashfield
Sound Designer & Co-Composer

Tic Ashfield is a BAFTA Cymru award-winning composer and sound designer living in South Wales.

Training: Royal Welsh College of Music and Drama.

Theatre and Dance: *Pigeon, Pryd Mae'r Haf?, Tir Sir Gar* (Theatr Genedlaethol Cymru); *The Boy With Two Hearts* (Wales Millennium Centre and National Theatre); *The Crash Test, You O.K.?* and *Metamorphosis* (Hijinx); *Anthem, The Invisible Woman* (Wales Millennium Centre); *Rocket Launch Blaenavon* (TinShed Theatre); *Ghost Light* (Theatrau); *Sir Gâr:*

Ffwrnes; *Qwerin* (Osian Meilir); *Heart of Cardiff* (radio play series – Sherman Cymru); *Lung Water* (online – National Theatre Wales, Sherman Cymru and Chippy Lane Productions); *Constellation Street* (online – National Theatre Wales, Sherman Cymru and The Other Room); *Ripples* (online – National Theatre Wales, Sherman Theatre and RWCMD); *A Number, All But Gone, The Awkward Years, American Nightmare, The Story* and *Hela* (The Other Room); *The Gathering, {150}, The Tide Whisperer, For as Long as the Heart Beats and Storm III* (National Theatre Wales); *On Bear Ridge* (National Theatre Wales and the Royal Court); *Dear to Me | Annwyl i mi* (National Dance Company Wales); *Peeling* (Taking Flight); *Cracked* (Pontardawe Arts Centre); *Blue* (Chippy Lane Productions); *Bottom* (Willy Hudson); *Richard III, Henry VI* and *Romeo and Juliet* (Omidaze Productions); *Saturday Night Forever* (Joio); *Momentos of Leaving, Moment(o)s for Elaine Paton; Hard Times* (Lighthouse); *Cold Rolling* (Ballet Cymru); and *My People* (Gwyn Emberton Dance).

TV and Film: *The Light in the Hall | Y Golau, Bregus, Hel Y Mynydd, Pili Pala, Hidden | Craith, Hinterland | Y Gwyll, Galesa, Andrew Marr: Great Scots* and *The Girl in the Diary.*

Nadine Rennie CDG
Casting Director

Nadine was in-house Casting Director at Soho Theatre for over fifteen years; working on new plays by writers including Dennis Kelly,

Bryony Lavery, Arinzé Kene, Roy Williams, Philip Ridley, Laura Wade, Hassan Abdulrazzak, Vicky Jones and Oladipo Agboluaje.

Since going freelance in January 2019 Nadine has worked for theatres across London and the UK including Arcola Theatre, Orange Tree Theatre, Sheffield Crucible, Leeds Playhouse, Paines Plough, Fuel Theatre, National Theatre of Wales, Northern Stage, Pleasance Theatre London, Almeida, Lyric, Hampstead and Minack theatres.

And continues to cast on a regular basis for Soho Theatre.

Recent and upcoming Theatre work: *He Said She Said* (Synergy Theatre Project & Kiln Theatre); *Leaves of Glass* (Park Theatre, Lidless Theatre); *Breeding* (Kings Head Theatre); *Agatha* (Theatre 503); *Further Than The Furthest Thing* (Minack Theatre, Cornwall).

Television: BAFTA-winning CBBC series *Dixi* (Series 1-3).

Nadine is a member of the Casting Directors Guild.

Alice Eklund
Associate
Director

Training: Aberystwyth University

Theatre: As Director – *Anthem* (Wales Millennium Centre); *The Amazing Adventures of Little Red* (Wales Millennium Centre / Sherman Theatre); *Bratiaith &*

See For Yourself; Maryland (Sherman Theatre).

As Associate / Assistant Director:
Tales of the Brothers Grimm (Sherman Theatre); *L'Assommoir & Canu'r Pwnc* (August012); *Ceilidh* (Goodspeed/HARTT School); *HELA, The Violence Series Tour & The Awkward Years* (The Other Room); *A Night in the Clink* (Papertrail).

Dollie Henry MBE
Movement
Director

Training: Laine Theatre Arts, London.

Theatre: West End Musicals:
Sophisticated Ladies (Gielgud Theatre); *King the Musical* (Piccadilly Theatre); *Stop the World I Want To Get Off* (Lyric Theatre); *Angels from America* (Shaftesbury Theatre); *Tribute To Sammy Davis Jr* (Theatre Royal, Drury Lane); *The Russ Abbot Madhouse Show* (The Palladium). *Helene in Sweet Charity* (UK Tour); *Hold Tight it's 60's Night* (UK Tour); *The Crucible* playing the role of Tituba (Royal Theatre – Northampton).

As a Choreographer & Director:
Sweet Lorraine (Old Fire Station Theatre, Oxford); *Ain't Misbehavin'* (The Verin English Theatre, Frankfurt); The musical *Ragged Child & Aladdin* (Theatre Royal, Northampton); *Salsa Celestina* (Palace Theatre, Watford); The musical *Big Nose, Cinderella & Snow White* (Belgrade Theatre, Coventry);

Up Against The Wall (Tricycle Theatre, London); *Blues Brother, Soul Sister*; (The Bristol Old Vic); *Tribute To Sammy Davis Jr,* (Theatre Royal, Drury Lane); *The Russ Abbot Madhouse Show* (The Palladium & National Tour); *Sophisticated Ladies* – Lyric Theatre (now Gielgud), London. *Godspell* (Tour), *Oh What A Lovely War* (Cochrane Theatre); *Oliver* (Giant Olive Productions); *King the Musical Concert* (Hackney Empire). Choreographer & co-director for *Inner City Jam* (Cockpit Theatre).

Film & TV: *Jingle Jangles* (Netflix); *Finding Your Feet; Knights & Emeralds* (Enigma Films); The Girl in *'Memories in Mind'* (BBC Documentary); *The Tales of Anansi* (Carlton TV); *The Russ Abbott Madhouse* (BBC); *The Leo Sayer Show* (BBC); *The Royal Variety/ Command Performances; The BAFTA Awards* (BBC).

In addition, Dollie is Founder/Artistic Director of BOP Jazz Theatre Company (BOP). Dance Theatre Lecturer and choreographer at Trinity Laban Conservatoire, PPA Guildford, Mountview Academy. Patron of The Hammond School Cheshire, Impact Dance Company and International Dance Teachers Association (IDTA).

Awards: In 2022 Dollie was awarded with an MBE for Services to Dance.

Ingrid Mackinnon
Intimacy
Co-ordinator

Ingrid Mackinnon is a movement director, choreographer, intimacy co- ordinator, teacher and dancer.

As intimacy co ordinator, her work for theatre includes *Phaedra* (National Theatre); *Super High Resolution* (Soho Theatre); *Enough of Him* (National Theatre of Scotland); *Girl on an Altar* (Kiln Theatre).

Intimacy support for theatre includes Carousel and as a Season Associate at Regent's Park in 2022.

Movement direction includes *Trouble In Butetown* (Donmar Warehouse); *Enough of Him* (National Theatre of Scotland); *A Dead Body In Taos* (Fuel Theatre); *The Darkest Part of the Night* (Kiln Theatre); *Girl on an Altar* (Kiln Theatre); *Playboy of the West Indies* (Birmingham Rep); *The Meaning of Zong* (Bristol Old Vic/ UK Tour); *Moreno* (Theatre503); *Red Riding Hood* (Theatre Royal Stratford East); *Antigone* (Mercury Theatre); *Romeo and Juliet* (Regent's Park Open Air Theatre - winner Black British Theatre Awards 2021 Best Choreography); *Liminal – Le Gateau Chocolat* (King's Head Theatre); *Liar Heretic Thief* (Lyric Hammersmith); *Reimagining Cacophony* (Almeida Theatre); *First Encounters: The Merchant Of Venice, Kingdom Come* (RSC); *Josephine* (Theatre Royal Bath); *Typical* (Soho Theatre); *#WeAreArrested* (Arcola Theatre and RSC); *The Border* (Theatre Centre); *Fantastic*

Mr. Fox (as Associate Movement Director, Nuffield Southampton and National/International tour); *Hamlet, #DR@CULA!* (Royal Central School of Speech and Drama); *Bonnie & Clyde* (UWL: London College of Music).

Pádraig Cusack
Producer

Education: Trinity College Dublin (Taylor Scholar); Royal Northern College of Music, Manchester.

Theatre: *Our Generation* (National Theatre/Chichester Festival); *Psychodrama* (Edinburgh Fringe/ Traverse Theatre); *The Boy with Two Hearts* (Wales Millennium Centre/National Theatre); *The Mirror Crack'd* (NCPA Mumbai); *Long Day's Journey into Night* (BAM New York & LA); *The Mirror Crack'd* (Wales Millennium Centre, UK & Ireland Tour); *Man to Man* (Wales Millennium Centre, Edinburgh, UK Tour, BAM New York); *A Girl is a Half-formed Thing* (Edinburgh Festival, UK Tour, London, New York); *Not I/Footfalls/Rockaby* (Royal Court, West End London, New York, Hong Kong & Perth Festivals, Paris); *Tiger Bay the Musical* (Wales Millennium Centre, Cape Town & Cardiff); *riverrun* (World Tour including London, New York, Adelaide & Sydney); *One Man, Two Guvnors* (National Theatre, UK Tour, AustralAsia Tour, Broadway); *John Gabriel Borkman* (Abbey Theatre, BAM New York); *The Pitmen Painters* (National Theatre, UK Tour, West End & Broadway); *Phèdre* (National Theatre, Epidaurus Greece & Kennedy Center Washington DC); *Waves* (National Theatre, Luxembourg, Salzburg Festival & Lincoln Center New York); *Primo* (National Theatre, Baxter Theatre Cape Town & Broadway); *Happy Days* (National Theatre, World Tour including Dublin Festival, Holland Festival, Festival de Otoño Madrid, Kennedy Center Washington DC & BAM New York); *The History Boys* (National Theatre, UK Tour, Hong Kong Festival, Australia/NZ Tour, Broadway) and *The Servant of Two Masters* (WYP, Venice).

Opera: *La Voix Humaine* (Wales Millennium Centre, Aldeburgh Festival, UK).

Dance: *Play Without Words* (New Adventures, London, Moscow & Tokyo); *Rian* (Fabulous Beast, Sadlers Wells); *Bennelong* (Bangarra Dance Theatre, Sydney).

Television: *My Country* (BBC); *She Stoops to Conquer* (Heritage).

Event: *we're here because we're here* (Jeremy Deller, 1418 Now, UK-wide).

Awards: Olwen Wymark Writers' Guild of Great Britain Award 2023.

Music Acknowledgements:
With thanks to Jean Adebambo, Lizz Wright.

CANOLFAN MILENIWM CYMRU

Cartref creadigol i bawb

Rydyn ni'n tanio'r dychymyg drwy groesawu sioeau, digwyddiadau a phrofiadau o'r radd flaenaf i Gymru – o theatr gerdd, comedi a dawns arobryn i sioeau cabaret sy'n torri tir newydd.

Rydyn ni'n creu ein cynyrchiadau ein hunain, gan arddangos straeon a doniau Cymru yn rhyngwladol ac yn ddigidol, ac rydyn ni'n cydweithio â phobl ifanc, cymunedau ac artistiaid i sicrhau y gall pawb fod yn greadigol a dysgu sgiliau newydd.

Fel elusen, rydyn ni'n ennyn angerdd dros y celfyddydau gyda phrofiadau dysgu sy'n newid bywydau a chyfleoedd i ddisgleirio.

Os hoffech chi ein cefnogi ni gyda'n hamcanion i ysbrydoli cenedlaethau'r dyfodol, meithrin talent a gweithio gyda chymunedau i ehangu mynediad rhad ac am ddim i'r celfyddydau, ewch i **wmc.org.uk/cefnogwchni**

NI YW CANOLFAN MILENIWM CYMRU. TANWYDD I'R DYCHYMYG.

WALES MILLENNIUM CENTRE

A creative home for everyone

We fire imaginations by welcoming world-class shows, events and experiences to Wales – from critically acclaimed musical theatre, comedy and dance to intimate, ground-breaking cabaret.

We create our own productions, showcasing Welsh stories and talent internationally and digitally, and we work with young people, communities and artists, to ensure everyone can be creative and learn new skills.

As a charity, we ignite a passion for the arts with life-changing learning experiences and chances to shine in the spotlight.

To support us in our aims of inspiring future generations, nurturing talent and working with communities to expand free access to the arts, visit **wmc.org.uk/support**

WE ARE WALES MILLENNIUM CENTRE. FIRE FOR THE IMAGINATION.

**CANOLFAN MILENIWM CYMRU
WALES MILLENNIUM CENTRE**

wmc.org.uk

ES & FLO

Jennifer Lunn

For my grandmothers

Esmeé Lunn 1916–1976
Florence Maureen Small 1927–2012

Characters

ES, *early seventies, white*
FLO, *sixty to sixty-five, Black*
BEATA, *thirty, white, Polish*
KASIA, *eight, mixed heritage*
CATHERINE, *fifty, white*

Setting

Cardiff, Wales

Time

2023

Note on the Dialogue

Where text is in [square brackets] these words are not necessarily spoken. They are there to show the intention of the line.

Where a line starts or ends with / it is an interruption.

This text went to press before the end of rehearsals and so may differ slightly from the play as performed.

Scene One

Lights up on an open-plan kitchen/living room. There is a kitchen table and a sofa. There is a an entrance via the front door, and a back door in the kitchen. There is a bottle of milk on the kitchen table.

The radio is playing. ES *enters. She appears to be the perfect representation of a retired schoolteacher. She is seventy-one years old today.*

There is something on the radio related to the Conservative party.

ES. Fucking Tories.

> ES *turns the radio off. She looks around. She is wandering slightly.*
>
> *She eventually makes her way to a sweet tin which she takes to the sofa and sits with. She opens the tin and takes out a bag of Jelly Babies and a birthday card.*
>
> *She looks at the card briefly, smiles and puts it on the coffee table. She opens the Jelly Babies and eats one, biting the head off it first.*
>
> FLO *enters through the front door and calls. She is a Black woman in her early sixties.*

FLO. Hello.

ES. Flo.

FLO. Close your eyes!

ES. Why?

FLO. I've got a surprise. I just need a minute.

ES. –

FLO. Are they closed?

ES. Yes.

> ES *sits with eyes closed as* FLO *gets out a birthday cake in a box. She takes it out of its box, quickly opens a packet of birthday candles that she has in her pocket, puts them into the cake and tries to light them. This is harder than she'd like.*

Can I look yet?

FLO. No! Wait.

> ES *hears the lighter.*

ES. Are you smoking?

FLO (*laughing*). No. Keep them closed.

ES. What are you doing?

FLO. Wait. Nearly ready… Okay… Open them. (*Singing.*) Happy Birthday to you, Happy Birthday to you, Happy Birthday dear Esmee, Happy Birthday to you!

> ES *moves to the kitchen and looks at the cake with delight.*

ES. Flo /

FLO. Make a wish.

ES. I wish…

FLO. Don't say it. Just wish and blow. Before the wax drips on the cake.

> ES *shuts her eyes for a moment then opens them, blows out the candles. She looks at* FLO *with a smile.*

ES. I always wish the same thing. Thank you.

FLO. Happy birthday. Seventy-one!

ES. Well, I don't feel it. A bit of life in me yet I hope.

FLO. Plenty! Hang on…

> FLO *plays a song on a CD player.*

ES and FLO. Tune!

ES. Oh, I love this song.

FLO. Come on, birthday girl!

> FLO *starts to sing to and dance with* ES. *They end up with a flamboyant dip, laughing.*

> Still got it!

ES. Not bad for an old girl!

FLO. You're as young as the woman you feel.

ES. Lucky me then.

> *She grabs* FLO. *They laugh. A kiss.*

FLO. Right. Cake?

ES. Why not.

FLO. You do the tea. I'll cut the cake.

ES. Alright then.

> FLO *gets plates and a knife and takes them to the table.* ES *stands for a moment in the kitchen. She has forgotten why she is there. She turns off the music.* FLO *looks up.*

FLO. What's wrong?

ES. Oh, nothing. Couldn't hear myself think.

> *Beat.* ES *is still.*

FLO. Do you want me to do the tea?

ES. I'm doing it.

> ES *puts the kettle on and gets the pot ready.* FLO *takes the candles out of the cake and cuts two slices.*

FLO. Did the post come? Were there any birthday cards?

ES. No.

> *The kettle boils.* FLO *looks at* ES *expectantly.*

> What?

FLO. The tea.

ES. Yes, yes. I'm doing it.

ES fills the teapot and brings it to the table and sits. There are no cups.

FLO. I'll get some cups, shall I?

ES. Oh sorry, what was I thinking?

FLO. I'll get them.

FLO goes to get cups.

ES. This cake is lovely. Is it from the place by your work?

FLO. I don't work at the library any more.

ES. Oh no. Sorry, love.

FLO. It's okay.

FLO returns with cups and pours the tea.

There we go.

ES. Well, cheers! Happy Birthday!

FLO does not correct her.

FLO. Yes. Happy Birthday.

They both sip tea and eat cake.

ES. Lovely.

FLO looks around and notices the card on the coffee table.

FLO. Who's that card from?

ES gets up and goes and gets the card. She looks at it as she comes back to the table.

ES. It's from Peter.

ES puts it on the table. FLO picks it up.

FLO. Did it come today? You said no post came. 'Dear Mum, Happy Birthday, love from Peter and Catherine'. Is that it?

FLO *shakes her head, disappointed but not surprised.*

Es?

ES. Yes?

FLO. Why didn't you say this came?

ES. I don't know.

FLO. Did you think I would /

ES. Your tea is getting cold.

They sit quietly drinking tea and eating cake. They are both thinking. FLO has something she wants to say but can't find the words.

They catch each other's eyes and smile.

Thank you. This is lovely.

Pause.

FLO *has an air of fake casualness. They have had this conversation many times before.*

FLO. Did you have a chance to look at the papers?

ES. What?

FLO. It doesn't matter if not. We just said we might look at them today. Not getting any younger!

ES. Thanks!

FLO. Do you know what? It's your birthday. I'm sorry. We'll look at them another day.

FLO *reaches out and holds ES's hand.*

ES. It's okay.

FLO. You sure?

ES. Of course.

FLO *smiles and goes to get some forms from the side. She comes back to the table with them.*

FLO. So, this one's for you and this one's for me.

ES reads the forms.

ES. Power of attorney?

FLO. Yes.

ES. I didn't know that was what you meant.

She puts the forms down.

FLO. Es. We can't keep putting this off.

ES. But this is for married couples.

This hurts.

FLO. Or children or /

ES. Peter?

FLO. Well…

ES. He's my next of kin.

FLO. And when did he last come to see you?

ES. He was here on my birthday.

FLO. Three years ago.

Something flashes across ES's face but she doesn't say anything. She is still reading the forms. FLO is watching her.

If I got ill, wouldn't you want to be able to /

ES. You're not ill, are you?

FLO. No.

ES. Good.

FLO. But…

ES. I don't see how we can do this. We're not…

FLO. We just need someone to sign and say that we… We've talked about this, Es.

ES looks up.

ES. And how do I explain it to Peter?

A stand-off.

FLO. Well. Maybe it's time to /

ES. No.

FLO. But...

ES. You promised.

FLO. But that was /

ES. He's my son.

FLO. Fine.

FLO *gathers up the papers, gets up and puts them back in the drawer.* ES *watches her.*

ES. I love you.

FLO *goes upstairs.*

ES *stands for a moment and then starts to clear away the stuff on the table. She puts the cake back into its box, puts the cups and plates and the teapot by the sink. The milk stays on the table.*

The doorbell rings. She goes to answer it.

BEATA. Hello, Mrs Turner?

ES. Yes. Hello.

BEATA. I'm sorry I am a bit late.

ES. Come in. What a nice surprise.

ES *re-enters with* BEATA *and* KASIA. BEATA *is a striking-looking young Polish woman.* KASIA *is her mixed-heritage, eight-year-old daughter.*

Flo! We have guests.

BEATA. Flo is your friend, yes? Is she here?

ES. Flo!

FLO *comes downstairs and enters. She has been crying.*

FLO. Oh! Es?

BEATA. I'm Beata. The agency sent me. Hello.

FLO. Sorry?

BEATA. You were not expecting me today? The agency definitely said Monday.

FLO. The agency?

BEATA. Yes! You are Flo, yes?

FLO. Yes.

BEATA. Okay.

FLO. Sorry, who are you?

BEATA. I'm sorry. This is my daughter Kasia. It's school holidays and her friend is sick so she couldn't go to his house. Normally I wouldn't. She won't /

ES (*to* KASIA). What's your name?

BEATA. Kasia.

ES. I'm Esmee. How old are you?

BEATA. She's eight.

KASIA. I'm nearly nine.

ES. Would you like a Jelly Baby?

　　ES *looks at* BEATA *to check.*

BEATA. Just one, Kasia.

　　ES *offers the Jelly Babies to* KASIA *who takes one.*

KASIA. Thank you.

ES. Orange. Good choice. I like to bite their heads off!

　　ES *takes a Jelly Baby from the tin, bites its head off and shows it to* KASIA.

FLO. Es, why didn't you tell me about this?

ES. Oh, I don't know. You know me, brain like a sieve these days. Sorry. Would you make us some tea?

FLO is a bit baffled but heads to the kitchen.

BEATA. Kasia, some reading, okay?

KASIA takes a book out of her backpack.

ES. *Pippi Longstocking*? How wonderful? Come on then.

ES gestures for KASIA to sit with her on the sofa. KASIA sits.

BEATA. Mrs Turner? You don't need to /

ES. You can call me Esmee. Now, I haven't heard this book in a long time. Don't worry about us, Mum. Flo will make you some tea.

KASIA sits down next to ES and starts to read.

FLO. I'm sorry, I didn't mean to be rude earlier. I didn't know you were coming.

BEATA takes her coat off and is looking for something to do.

BEATA. Oh, that's fine. Can I help? Shall I wash up these cups and plates?

FLO. God, no!

BEATA. It's what I'm here for. I might as well get started while...

She gestures at ES and KASIA.

FLO. Sorry?

BEATA. I'm only booked for an hour today so put me to work.

FLO. –

BEATA. Unless Esmee had something else in mind. I can change sheets or do ironing.

FLO. I'm sorry. I'm a little bit confused. You're here for tutoring, right?

BEATA laughs.

BEATA. No, I'm from Kind Living. I'm here to help Esmee, you know. Sorry. You want to see paperwork?

BEATA *gets paperwork from her bag and hands it to* FLO. FLO *checks the paperwork for* BEATA*'s name and pronounces it unsurely.*

FLO. I'm sorry, Beata?

BEATA. Beata.

FLO. We didn't know anything about this. What's going on?

BEATA. Esmee's son was worried about her and so Mrs Turner – Catherine? – arranged for me to come.

FLO. But Peter hasn't... not since the pandemic. Why would he...?

BEATA. I'm sorry, I don't know the details. I was told he visited two weeks ago, and didn't think she was managing on her own. Apparently he agreed it all with her. But perhaps she doesn't [remember]...

FLO *goes to the sofa.* BEATA *heads to the kitchen; getting her bearings.*

FLO. Es, have you spoken to Peter?

ES. Peter? I saw him on my birthday!

FLO. Today is your birthday.

ES. He brought me a card.

FLO. Brought or sent?

ES. Brought. And these Jelly Babies.

FLO. Where's the envelope?

ES *hands* FLO *the envelope which just says 'Mum' on the front.*

He was here?

ES. Yes. I told you.

FLO. When?

ES. I don't know. We're reading Flo!

ES goes back to reading with KASIA. FLO *stares at the envelope, her mind racing.*

FLO (*to herself*). Shit.

FLO turns back and BEATA *has found the teapot and tea bags.*

BEATA. Cups?

FLO. Oh.

BEATA. It's fine, I'll just wash them…

FLO. No, you don't have to.

BEATA. It's fine. This is what I'm here for.

FLO. –

BEATA fills the teapot. FLO *looks on suspiciously, baffled by this woman in her kitchen. She looks over at* ES, *uneasily, and back at* BEATA*'s paperwork and ID again.*

So you…

BEATA. I work for Kind Living. We offer care and assistance for people like Esmee.

FLO. People like Esmee?

BEATA. Yes. I help out with things like shopping /

FLO. I do the shopping.

BEATA. Cooking.

FLO. I do all that.

BEATA. Okay. Well, I can help here in the house, take Esmee out, talk and chat, you know. Give you some time for yourself.

FLO. I don't need time for myself.

BEATA. Flo. It's okay I call you Flo?

FLO. Actually /

KASIA. Mum? Can I have another sweet?

BEATA. One more. Esmee, I'm making tea.

ES. Lovely.

> ES *and* KASIA *have another Jelly Baby each. ES bites the head off first. This time* KASIA *does the same and then continues to read.*

FLO. This is absurd. Who do I call to /

> FLO *gets out a mobile.*

BEATA. Look. I'm sorry. It really is Esmee I'm here to talk to. See what help she needs.

> BEATA *goes to the fridge.*

FLO. She doesn't need any help and she certainly doesn't need a strange woman making herself at home in our kitchen.

> BEATA *stops and looks at* FLO.

BEATA. Mrs…

FLO. *Miss.* Carter.

> BEATA *starts pouring tea.*

BEATA. Miss Carter. I'm sorry. I know you're Esmee's friend and I don't mean to be rude but… it really isn't up to you.

> FLO *goes to reply but has to bite her tongue.*

> This has been arranged by Esmee's son. I won't get in the way. You can just think of me as /

> KASIA *and* ES *laugh.* FLO *and* BEATA *turn to look.* FLO *watches* ES. ES*'s happiness softens the difficulty of the moment.*

> Esmee, could we have a chat, please?

ES. We need to finish this chapter first. Flo will look after you.

BEATA. Just to the end of the chapter, Kasia, okay?

BEATA *comes back to the kitchen.*

She's strict!

FLO *does not join in the joke.* BEATA *sits at the table and pours her and* FLO *tea.* FLO *does not sit.*

Have some tea, Miss Carter.

BEATA *gets out a notebook and pen.*

Can you tell me some things about Esmee? You know her a long time?

FLO. Forty years.

BEATA. Old friends. Wow, long time. Work?

FLO. We met at Greenham.

BEATA. Greenham?

FLO. The peace camp.

BEATA. ?

FLO. 1980s? Nuclear weapons? Thousands of women surrounding an army base?

BEATA. ?

FLO. Jesus!

Why do you need to know all this anyway?

BEATA. It helps me to get to know Esmee. It's useful to have familiar things to talk about.

KASIA *calls out.*

KASIA. Finished the chapter, Mum.

BEATA *goes over to* ES.

BEATA. Esmee, can we have a chat please?

ES. Of course. She reads very well.

BEATA. Thank you.

KASIA. Can I play on your phone, Mum?

BEATA *gives* KASIA *her phone.*

BEATA. Headphones. Esmee, why don't you come and sit with us?

ES *comes to the table and she and* BEATA *sit.* FLO *is left standing.*

ES. Has Flo been looking after you?

BEATA. Yes. Would you like some tea?

ES. Thank you. Flo, some cake. It's my birthday. Flo bought me a lovely cake. I bet the little one would like some cake.

BEATA. It's your birthday? Today? I'm sorry, Catherine didn't say.

We shouldn't eat your birthday cake.

ES. Shush – There's only us two.

FLO *is bringing the cake over on napkins.* ES *throws her a look.*

Flo, plates.

FLO *rolls her eyes but does as she is asked.*

BEATA. How lovely. May I ask how old you are, Esmee? If it isn't rude.

ES. Not at all, I am seventy-one. But I'm told I don't look it!

BEATA. Not at all.

ES. A slice for the little one?

BEATA. Kasia!

KASIA *can't hear.*

Don't worry.

ES. Can't have her being left out. Flo.

ES *gestures to* FLO *to take a slice* KASIA.

BEATA. That's very kind. Do you have any grandchildren, Esmee?

FLO *takes the cake to* KASIA. *She looks at* KASIA*'s hair disapprovingly.*

ES. No. (*Slightly whispered.*) I don't think Catherine could.

BEATA. I'm sorry.

FLO. Some cake?

KASIA. Thank you.

BEATA. Am I right that you are a widow?

ES. An old widow!

BEATA. Your husband passed?

FLO *returns to the table.*

FLO. Ex-husband.

ES. Jim? Oh yes, he died.

FLO. Es, Catherine thinks you need help. I was telling... Beata... that you are okay.

ES. Oh yes, all fine here. I'm a lady of leisure these days, aren't I, Flo?

BEATA. Do you cook, Esmee?

ES. I was never much in the kitchen. My husband was always very disappointed about that.

FLO. We /

BEATA. So what do you get up to?

ES. This and that. We walk a lot. I do the garden. I have my students.

BEATA. And how is your memory, Esmee? If you don't mind me asking.

FLO. Is this some kind of assessment?

ES. I was always forgetting where I'd put my glasses but Flo bought me this string.

BEATA. I need one of those for my keys!

ES. Now, some cake for the little one?

ES goes to cut another slice of cake.

FLO. You've already given her some.

BEATA catches FLO's eye.

ES. Oh yes, of course. Sorry!

BEATA. That's okay.

FLO. This is ridiculous. I'm sorry. Who do we call to…?

ES (*gesturing to* KASIA). What's her name?

BEATA. Kasia.

ES. Kasia. Well, you must bring her round again. What do you say, Flo?

There is a subtle gesture of physical familiarity from ES to FLO, which BEATA clocks and she begins to understand they are more than friends.

FLO. Okay.

ES. A slice of cake for…

BEATA. Kasia.

ES. Kasia. Right.

ES cuts another slice of cake and takes it to KASIA. FLO watches her – worried.

It's my birthday.

KASIA. Penblwydd Hapus.

ES. Oh, diolch. Ooh. Can I play?

KASIA gives ES one of her headphones and they look at the game together.

FLO *is silent. Her mind is racing, this situation is slipping out of her control.*

BEATA*'s tone has shifted slightly with her understanding of their relationship.*

BEATA. When did she start forgetting things?

It can be hard to tell sometimes when you are living with someone.

FLO. We're getting older. Forgetfulness comes with the territory.

BEATA. It's more than that though, isn't it?

ES *and* KASIA *laugh.*

They seem to have made friends.

FLO. She's at her best with kids.

Pause.

BEATA. It's all paid for. Three times a week, two hours each time. We can arrange when is a good time. I'm very flexible.

FLO. –

BEATA. It's hard, I know. To ask for help.

FLO. She doesn't need help.

BEATA. No, but perhaps some 'homework' might do her good.

FLO. Can you bring her every time?

BEATA. Well, I'll need to check with the agency but /

FLO. Like tutoring?

BEATA. I suppose.

FLO. And you can tell Catherine /

BEATA. Miss Carter, I

FLO. You can tell Catherine that Esmee's fine.

*The scene ends and there is a transition sequence – the
beginnings of what looks like family with ES at the centre
and FLO cautiously at the sidelines. Naturalistic but
choreographed. The sounds of Greenham.*

Scene Two

ES *and* KASIA *are sat at the table doing* KASIA*'s homework.*
BEATA *and* CATHERINE *are at the front door.*

CATHERINE. I wanted to see how things were going. The
agency said you'd be here this afternoon.

BEATA. Flo has gone to Tesco's.

CATHERINE. Yes, I think I just saw her leaving. It's Esmee I'm
here to… Oh, who's that?

BEATA. My daughter Kasia. It's all been agreed.

CATHERINE. Oh yes.

KASIA. Fifteen divided by five… Four?

ES. Don't just guess. You have to sort them into groups.

CATHERINE. Esmee?

ES *doesn't look up but raises a finger to* CATHERINE.

ES. Sh-Sh. Just a few more to do.

CATHERINE *is affronted.*

CATHERINE. Oh!

CATHERINE *is about to try again.*

ES *opens a bag of Jelly Babies. They use the Jelly Babies to
work out the sums.*

BEATA. Better not to interrupt her.

CATHERINE. It's just /

BEATA. She can get a bit confused. They won't be long. Tea?

CATHERINE moves away from ES and KASIA, and speaks to BEATA almost conspiratorially.

CATHERINE. Not for me. I've come to talk to Esmee about what happens next. My husband and I have been trying to find her somewhere closer to us. You know, some kind of 'assisted living'? Is that what they call it?

BEATA. Yes, but /

CATHERINE. It is a three-hour drive from London to Cardiff. It's very difficult for Peter.

BEATA. She would like to see him more. She talks about him a lot.

CATHERINE. That's nice. But it's proving difficult. I'm sure you know, it's virtually impossible to find a good place with spaces. The ones we found... Well, they're just awful. The staff barely speak any... Well, you know.

BEATA reacts perceptibly. CATHERINE attempts a save.

The agency says it has been going terribly well here. What is it, a couple of months now?

BEATA. I don't think she needs to move.

CATHERINE. Oh no, we'll definitely move her. It's just more complicated than we thought. We need Esmee's consent for selling the house and...

BEATA. You want to sell the house?

CATHERINE. Yes.

BEATA. But this is Flo's house too?

CATHERINE. Oh no. Esmee took Flo in when she was... Well, down on her luck you might say.

BEATA. I really think you should speak to Flo.

CATHERINE. Look, you're obviously very fond of them both and that's great, but you said yourself – she's getting confused.

BEATA. Yes, but not so much. And moving would /

CATHERINE. Peter is all she's got.

KASIA. Finished! Can I have a sweet, Mum?

BEATA. Did she get them all right, Esmee?

ES. Of course! My little brain box! Jelly Babies all round.

CATHERINE *moves to the table.*

Hello. Jelly Baby?

CATHERINE. Not for me thank you, Esmee.

ES. Oh, go on. It won't kill you!

CATHERINE *takes a Jelly Baby and then looks at it not sure what to do with it.*

Where's Flo? She likes the green ones best.

BEATA. She's gone to Tesco's. She won't be long. A quick bit of reading, then she'll be back and we can eat. Will you stay, Catherine?

CATHERINE *quickly puts the Jelly Baby in her bag or pocket.*

CATHERINE. Esmee?

ES. Yes. Hello.

CATHERINE. I'm Catherine. Peter's wife.

ES. Yes, I know. I'm not stupid. Where's Peter?

CATHERINE. He's at work.

ES. Have you come to do some washing?

CATHERINE. What? Oh, it's a long time since we did that, Esmee.

ES *tries to cover her mistake.*

ES. I was joking.

CATHERINE. Of course. How have you been?

ES. Oh fine. These two keep an eye on me.

ES *smiles at* KASIA *who smiles back.*

CATHERINE. I'm glad it's been helpful having...

CATHERINE *can't remember* BEATA*'s name.*

them here.

BEATA. Shall I make tea?

CATHERINE. Which brings me to something else. We have found you a lovely place.

CATHERINE *pulls a leaflet out of her bag and proffers it to* ES *who doesn't take it.*

BEATA *starts making tea but does not take her eyes off* CATHERINE *for long.*

It's near us. We'd be able to see you more often. And Flo wouldn't have to worry about you so much.

ES. Oh, I don't want to be a worry.

CATHERINE (*talking to her like a child*). No, of course.

ES *takes the brochure and has a look. She's uncomfortable and wants to get back to reading.*

BEATA *goes to the fridge for milk. She can tell it is off just by looking.*

What do you think?

ES. It's very nice. I /

She tries to hand the brochure back and return to reading with KASIA *but* CATHERINE *leaps in.*

CATHERINE. Great! Great, great. You just need to sign these forms and we can organise everything.

CATHERINE *pulls LPA* (*lasting power of attorney*) *forms and a pen out of her bag and puts them in front of* ES.

ES *is unnerved by the papers.*

ES. Oh, I'd need my glasses for that small print and God knows where I've put them!

KASIA (*laughing*). They're round your neck!

CATHERINE. Don't worry, Peter and I have filled them all out for you. It's just a request for an LPA.

ES. Oh, acronyms! How is anyone supposed to understand anything if we stop using words?

BEATA. Sorry no milk. I could make some coffee?

CATHERINE. It means that we can take care of everything and get you moved in here as soon as possible.

KASIA. Are you moving?

ES. Moving? No, I'm not going anywhere. Now, what about this reading?

ES *passes the forms and the leaflet back to* CATHERINE.

CATHERINE. Esmee /

BEATA *comes to the table and takes the papers.*

BEATA. You can leave them with me. I help lots of clients with these forms so I know what I'm doing.

And it's so important that Esmee understands everything, isn't it? Who have you put down as the certificate provider?

CATHERINE. What?

BEATA *is thumbing through the pages.*

BEATA. The person who verifies that Es is...

(*Surprised.*) Flo? Oh, I don't think Flo can.

CATHERINE*'s mobile rings.*

CATHERINE. Why not?

She answers it. KASIA *is watching her.*

Peter... Yes, I'm there now... Yes... No, no, she's out...
Well no, but the Polish girl is going to get it all signed for us.
Well... She does this kind of thing a lot. It might be better if
it's... No... No... No... I know, but it's not that [easy]...

Peter is shouting and CATHERINE *moves moves away from
the kitchen.*

BEATA *is unnerved.*

KASIA. He doesn't sound very nice.

ES. No.

Peter hangs up on CATHERINE. *She tries to cover.*

CATHERINE. Sorry about that.

BEATA. Everything okay?

CATHERINE. Yes, fine. Peter is very stressed with work. He
runs his own business so...

BEATA. Oh. Right.

CATHERINE. I really need to get those forms signed. Can you
put them in the post tomorrow?

BEATA. I'm not back here till Friday.

CATHERINE. Friday then.

BEATA. I'll see what I can /

CATHERINE (*firmly*). / Friday.

BEATA *is slightly taken aback.* CATHERINE *goes back over
to the table and interrupts* KASIA*'s reading.* KASIA *stops
when* CATHERINE *looks at her.*

Esmee?

CATHERINE *has forgotten* BEATA*'s name and gestures to
her.*

BEATA. Beata.

CATHERINE. Yes. Beata will help you sign the forms when you're less busy. But I'll leave this with you to have a look at.

The front door opens and closes. BEATA *tries to catch* FLO *before she comes in.*

You'd have your own flat but you could still join in lots of activities.

FLO *comes straight past* BEATA. *She has one carrier bag with her.*

FLO. Catherine?

ES. Oh no. I'm fine here with Flo.

FLO. What's going on?

CATHERINE. But Beata says you get a bit confused sometimes.

FLO. What's going on, Catherine?

CATHERINE *turns. This was what she was hoping to avoid.*

CATHERINE. Hello, Flo. I was just saying to Esmee, it's been very kind of you looking after her all this time, but really you should have told us what was going on. Has she seen a doctor?

FLO. She's fine.

CATHERINE. I don't think she is.

CATHERINE *turns back to* ES *who is looking at the brochure with* KASIA.

KASIA. It's got a swimming pool. Cool!

CATHERINE. Oh yes, it's very swish. Not cheap, no, but you'll be well looked after and – (*Turning to* FLO.) Flo, you can relax, go back to… your family… wherever you are from perhaps?

FLO *is shocked by this comment.* CATHERINE *keeps going.*

You two have lived here for…?

FLO *moves to be closer to* ES.

FLO. Thirty-six years.

FLO stares at CATHERINE challengingly. CATHERINE is slightly unnerved.

CATHERINE. Yes, so I know it's a big change but... We'll arrange selling the house and, of course, we're not throwing you out straight away.

ES (*looking up*). Who's throwing who out?

FLO. Nobody is throwing anyone out.

FLO physically reassures ES in some way. CATHERINE clocks this but quickly returns to her purpose.

ES. Good. Now, we need to get on with this reading if you don't mind.

FLO and CATHERINE stare at each other over ES and KASIA. ES is uncomfortable and getting fractious.

Don't crowd us! The girl's trying to read for goodness' sake. Come on, sweetheart.

ES gets up and goes to the sofa. KASIA follows.

CATHERINE. Peter just wants what's best.

FLO. Well, maybe he should come and talk to his mother himself rather than sending you.

CATHERINE. He did. That's why...

She gestures to BEATA.

He found her here on her own, no idea what was what, no food in the fridge.

FLO. I /

CATHERINE. Look. I know it's difficult. You've obviously been a very good friend to her but it's time to let us take over now.

So, Esmee.

ES. Shh! Flo?

FLO. It's alright. Catherine is just leaving.

CATHERINE. Fine, but /

> FLO *hands her the brochure*.

FLO. And you can take this with you.

> CATHERINE *is forced to give in. She looks at* BEATA.

> FLO *is about to say something but* CATHERINE *catches her.*

CATHERINE. I'll let myself out.

> (*To* BEATA.) Friday.

> CATHERINE *goes and* FLO *watches.*

FLO. Shit!

BEATA. I'm so sorry, Flo, I couldn't /

FLO. Shit. Shit. Shit.

BEATA. –

FLO. They can't do this, can they?

BEATA. Well /

FLO. Have you said something to them?

BEATA. No.

FLO. Because if /

BEATA. Flo. Honestly.

FLO. Are they after the money?

BEATA. I don't /

FLO. Because he doesn't deserve a penny from her.

BEATA. –

FLO. And did you hear her? 'You can go back to where you came from!' Fucki– /

KASIA. Mum, I'm hungry.

> FLO *realises she's sworn in front of* KASIA.

FLO. Sorry. Fuck! Sorry!

BEATA. Is the shopping in the car?

FLO. Tesco's was packed. I got pizza.

KASIA. Yes!!

BEATA. You didn't get milk? Or bread?

FLO. I promised Kasia I'd do her hair tonight so I wanted to get back. I'll go tomorrow.

BEATA. But we're not here tomorrow.

FLO. I know.

BEATA. Maybe I could go to Tesco's for you now. Make sure you have a few things.

FLO *grabs the pizzas*.

FLO. Don't worry. It'll get cold. Here you go, Kasia.

KASIA *comes and gets a pizza from* FLO.

KASIA. Thanks, Flo.

FLO. Share it with Es.

KASIA. Look Es. Pizza.

ES. Ooooh.

FLO (*handing a pizza to* BEATA). Pepperoni.

BEATA. Flo. I am grateful for you feeding us and for helping with Kasia's hair, but...

FLO. What?

BEATA. I am here to make sure Esmee is okay /

FLO. She's fine.

BEATA. You can't live on takeaways.

FLO. Why not?

BEATA. The milk was off, I had to throw it away.

FLO. Are you on their side now?

BEATA. I'm not on anyone's side. I'm here to look after Esmee.

FLO. Because *I* can't?

BEATA. Flo!

FLO. We were managing fine before you /

BEATA. Okay, okay. I'm sorry. Let's eat. Then I'll make a list for shopping tomorrow.

FLO is a little broken by all of this. BEATA opens the pizza box for them to share. FLO looks at it and then gets up and gets a half-drunk bottle of wine from the side and a glass. She pours a glass and knocks it back in one go.

FLO. Wine, anyone? No? Just me then.

She pours another glass. She then sees the LPA forms on the side. She thinks at first they are her forms.

What are these doing...

BEATA. Catherine brought them.

FLO. What?!

BEATA. They're LPA forms.

FLO. I know what they are. Lasting power of bloody attorney. That sneaky bastard.

BEATA. It's not /

FLO. Jesus!

ES has got up, hearing FLO's raised voice.

ES. What's the matter, Flo?

FLO. Your bloody son. That's what's the matter!

ES. Flo! Little ears!

BEATA. Shall we talk about this after dinner?

FLO grabs a packet of tobacco from the side.

FLO. I'm not hungry. I'm going to have a cigarette.

She takes the forms and steps outside the back door. ES *calls after her.*

ES. Flo!

ES *looks back at* KASIA.

Never start smoking. Terrible habit.

KASIA. It makes your lungs rot. We learnt about it at school. We watched this video and they showed a lung that had gone all black and disgusting. It was really cool /

ES. Ooooh! /

BEATA. Kasia. Not while people are eating!

KASIA. And it will give you lung cancer which will kill you.

BEATA. Katarzyna! Proszę skupić się na jedzeniu.

KASIA. Sorry, Mum!

ES. Sorry, Mum!

ES *and* KASIA *giggle.* KASIA *is colouring in while eating her pizza off the coffee table.* BEATA *picks at the pizza glancing occasionally at the back door.*

FLO *comes back in.*

BEATA (*to* FLO). You okay?

FLO *gets another glass and offers it to* BEATA.

Flo, I… [shouldn't]

FLO. For me?

BEATA. Okay, but just the one.

FLO *pours two glasses. She is flicking through and finds the section she is supposed to sign.*

FLO. So, they get me to sign this to say she is capable of setting up the power of attorney. And then, what? Next week they decide she isn't capable any more and they swoop in and…? Fuck that.

FLO *goes to rip up the forms but* BEATA *grabs them.*

BEATA. Flo!

FLO. She's fine. So the milk's off. We're – (*She corrects herself quickly.*) She's managing.

FLO *starts to roll another cigarette.*

BEATA. May I?

FLO *offers her the tobacco.*

FLO. This is her home. This is where she needs to be. With [me] / her things, her life. Fucking Peter. And sending the 'little wife' to do his dirty work. Coward. But if he gets power of attorney then that's it, right? He's in charge and off she goes.

Come on – outside. I'm not allowed to smoke in the house.

FLO *and* BEATA *go outside the back door.*

Pause.

KASIA *moves from the sofa to the floor so that she can lean on the coffee table to do some drawing. She knocks* ES*'s leg as she moves.*

KASIA. Przepraszam.

ES. What was that?

KASIA. I said sorry. In Polish.

ES. You're Polish, I remember.

KASIA. Half-Polish.

ES. What's Poland like?

KASIA. I don't know. I've never been.

But… I'm saving up to buy us tickets. I looked on the internet and you can buy plane tickets to Poland for forty pounds each. I've saved up all my birthday and Christmas and pocket money for ages and I've got sixty pounds so far. I just need twenty more pounds and then I can surprise Mum.

ES. That's so nice.

KASIA suddenly looks at ES anxiously.

KASIA. You won't tell, will you?

ES. You are a lovely girl.

ES gets up and goes to an ornament. She lifts off a lid and pulls out twenty pounds. She looks round at KASIA as she puts the lid back on.

Don't tell Flo.

She winks at KASIA. She comes back to the sofa and she gives the twenty pounds to KASIA.

There you go.

KASIA's eyes are wide.

KASIA. Thank you!

She gives ES a huge hug and then tucks the twenty pounds safely into her book.

ES finds the picture.

ES. This is lovely. Who is it?

KASIA. It's you and Flo. I've drawn a big heart round you. Because you love each other.

Pause. ES is looking at the picture.

Are you married?

ES. Oh no. We've just lived together for a long time.

We did have a 'sort of' wedding though.

KASIA. When?

ES. Oh, a long time ago. We were much younger. It wasn't real but we had a great party… lots of dancing and singing… and a bonfire.

KASIA. Cool. Did you wear a dress?

ES. I did. Flo wore dungarees. She looked gorgeous.

KASIA. My friend Sam – his two mums got married and I was
a bridesmaid. Trish wore a dress and Fran wore a suit. She
looked really cool. I wore a red dress with stripy tights. It
was epic!

ES. Lovely.

KASIA. Why wasn't your wedding real though?

ES. What's that?

KASIA. Why wasn't your wedding real?

ES. I was already married and well, we're both women.

KASIA. Some girls marry girls – Get over it!

ES. Huh?

KASIA. Some girls marry girls – Get over it! Trish and Fran
have it on T-shirts. You should get married! Then I could be
your bridesmaid. I still have the tights.

ES. What?

> FLO *comes back in to get more wine.* KASIA *leans in close
> to* ES *and half-whispers.*

KASIA. Ask her. (*Calling to* FLO.) Flo?

> ES *and* KASIA *giggle.*

> Flo? Es wants to ask you something.

> FLO *comes over.*

FLO. Yes?

> KASIA *looks at* ES.

KASIA. Go on. Ask her.

ES. Ask her what?

> *She leans in again and whispers in her ear.*

> Don't be silly.

FLO. What?

KASIA. She wants to ask you to marry her. Cos your wedding was only a 'sort of wedding' and now two girls can get married.

I could be your bridesmaid… If you wanted.

FLO. Oh.

This is big.

BEATA *has come in and is now watching.*

KASIA. Did you really have a bonfire at your pretend wedding? I love bonfires. They smell nice.

FLO. Es?

KASIA. She said you had a bonfire and dancing and singing.

ES *starts to sing.*

ES. We are the Flo, we are the Es.
We are the weavers, we are the web.
We are the Flo, we are the Es.
We are the witches back from the dead.

ES *gets up and starts dancing.* KASIA *joins in singing.*

ES *takes* FLO*'s face in her hands and kisses her.*

FLO *is frozen. She looks at* BEATA.

KASIA. Come on, Es!

ES. Coming!

KASIA *pulls* ES *out of the room to take her upstairs.*

FLO *watches them go.*

BEATA. Flo.

FLO. I…

BEATA. I'm sorry. She /

FLO. No, no, it's not her fault. It's just…

BEATA. It's okay.

FLO. It's not. She... We don't...

BEATA. I know.

> FLO *realises what this means. She looks offstage.*

They'll be fine. They've built some kind of camp up there.

> FLO *still processing.*

More wine?

> FLO *looks at* BEATA *for a moment.*

BEATA. Flo?

FLO. Yeah.

> FLO *sits.* BEATA *pours* FLO *a glass of wine. She watches her for a moment just sat at the table. Eventually* BEATA *comes to the table.*

BEATA. Here.

> *They sit in silence.* FLO *drinks the wine.*

I understand.

FLO. Do you? I don't.

> *Pause.*

Did she tell you?

BEATA. No. I just...

FLO. ?

BEATA. You love each other. It is hard not to see that.

FLO. Why didn't you say anything?

BEATA. You didn't, so...

> FLO *is suddenly worried.*

FLO. Peter doesn't know. Or Catherine.

BEATA. It's okay. I haven't...

FLO *is relieved.*

FLO. Es just wouldn't. Couldn't.

BEATA *is listening.*

When I met her... She'd just left Jim and he was using anything he could to stop her from seeing Peter. She was fighting for custody and I didn't want her to lose her family like I'd lost mine... Not that it worked. Loads of Greenham women lost their kids. 'Unfit' they called them. We thought maybe when Peter was older we'd be able to...

But then she was teaching and they brought in fucking Section 28...

BEATA. Sorry?

FLO. It was this law. Teachers weren't allowed to 'promote' homosexuality.

BEATA *nods. She understands.*

She'd have lost her job.

I mean, I'd go to Pride on my own but she just couldn't.

And then she was made head and... I don't know. There was always another reason.

I suppose you think we're stupid.

BEATA. No.

Beat.

It's difficult. With family.

Can I tell you something?

FLO *nods.*

My parents don't know about Kasia. They are Catholic. Very strict. They would... Anyway. So, I don't tell them.

FLO. But...

BEATA. They are in Poland. They don't travel. Then Covid...

FLO. But she's their grandchild. They would love her.

BEATA. They are very... traditional.

FLO. By which you mean racist?

BEATA *shakes her head.*

BEATA. It's very different there. If they found out I had a child, on my own. That would...

FLO. ?

BEATA. I was twenty-one. It was just one night.

That kind of thing does not happen where I'm from. They would never speak to me again.

FLO. Yeah. I know all about that. Apparently I'm an abomination unto the Lord... A disgrace.

BEATA. Oh Boże!

FLO. I wasn't going to take that from people who are supposed to...

So, yeah. It is hard with family.

Easier to just...

BEATA. Yes. But, Flo. I think now you *have* to tell. If you don't, they'll...

FLO. She won't.

She doesn't want to let him down.

Beat.

BEATA. She told Kasia.

FLO. Yeah.

BEATA. And if Catherine and Peter know then everything is different.

FLO. Is it?

BEATA. Of course.

Pause. BEATA *looks at the time.*

Talk to her.

Flo.

FLO. Okay.

BEATA. Okay.

(*Calling upstairs.*) Kasia! Time to go.

FLO *is staring into space.*

I know it's hard.

FLO. –

KASIA *is heard running down the stairs.*

BEATA. We'll see you Friday.

And shop.

FLO. Yes.

KASIA *runs in excitedly.*

KASIA. Flo! Flo! We made a bender!

BEATA. What?!

FLO. It's a tent.

KASIA. It's what they lived in at Greenham. Just plastic sheets and sticks.

We made ours out of blankets. It keeps falling down but it's still cool.

And we made these.

She holds up a drawing of a CND symbol and the words 'BAN THE BOMB'.

She starts to sing to the tune of 'Frére Jacques'.

We are women. We are women.
We are strong. We are strong.
We say no. We say no.
To the bomb. To the bomb.

BEATA. Too right! Sounds like you've been learning a lot.

Did you say goodbye to Esmee?

KASIA. Yeah. She's going to keep the tent up so we can play again on Friday.

(*To* FLO.) She said you might help fix it because you were the best at making benders.

FLO. Did she?

KASIA. And fires.

FLO. Right.

BEATA. Okay. Home time. Say goodbye to Flo.

KASIA. But…

FLO. We'll do your hair on Friday. I promise.

KASIA beams at FLO.

KASIA. Thanks, Flo.

BEATA. Come on then, my little feminist.

She looks at FLO.

Talk to her.

KASIA dances off, singing as she goes. BEATA *smiles at* FLO.

BEATA and KASIA *leave and we hear the front door close.*

Silence. FLO *is still.*

Her eye catches the forms on the table. She goes to a drawer and pulls out her own LPA forms and goes back to the table. She sits with a pen and starts to compare the two sets of forms. A deep breath.

ES *is coming downstairs singing the same song as* KASIA. FLO *gets up to stand between* ES *and the forms.*

ES *dances up to* FLO *and puts her arms around her.* FLO *slightly tenses at first but then slowly gives in. They kiss.*

FLO. I hear you built a tent.

ES. Barely! I never had your secret knack.

She smiles flirtatiously.

You were always so good with your hands.

FLO. Flirt.

They kiss.

You *were* always terrible with the benders.

ES. I was good at the floor.

(*With a twinkle.*) And the bed!

FLO. Oh God! All those bloody carrier bags you insisted on laying /

ES. I didn't want us to get muddy.

FLO. But they were so noisy whenever we rolled around.

ES. And there was a lot of rolling around.

They both smile knowingly.

FLO. There really was.

ES. I'd never known anything like it.

FLO. You were a quick learner.

ES. You were a very attentive teacher.

FLO. Leading you astray.

ES. Over the fence and straight into the arms of the police.

FLO. Not bad for a first date!

They both laugh.

ES. I was so excited.

FLO. Your first demo is always /

ES. It wasn't that.

FLO. ?

ES. It was you.

They kiss.

They stop and just look at each other. A moment of the old times. FLO *doesn't want it to end.*

Thank you.

FLO. What for?

ES. Everything you do.

FLO. Don't be /

ES. I'm forgetting things.

FLO. You /

ES. I am. Nothing but trouble, eh?

FLO. My kind of trouble!

ES *kisses* FLO.

Pause.

I need to talk to you about something.

ES. I can't promise to remember.

FLO. I'm serious.

ES. So am I.

FLO *takes a second and then goes for it.*

FLO. We have to talk to Peter about us.

The atmosphere changes immediately.

ES. No.

FLO. Es.

ES. No.

FLO. Just listen for a minute. Please?

ES. How many times?

FLO. Please! It's different now.

ES. Why?

FLO. Because you're right. You're forgetting. More than you
    think. I'm trying. I really am. But...

ES. But what?

FLO. He wants to move you to London.

ES. He won't. I'll talk to him.

FLO. They're trying to get power of attorney. They want to take
    you away. You saw how Catherine was today.

ES. Catherine?

FLO. Do you remember?

ES. Yes. Of course I do. We did some maths, some reading.
    She's so bright.

FLO. Not Kasia. Catherine. Peter's wife.

ES. Right.

FLO. Do you remember?

   ES *is getting flustered.*

ES. Is this some kind of interrogation?

FLO. Es, I'm trying to /

ES. I'm forgetful. I'm not a bloody idiot.

FLO. Es /

ES. I'm tired. I'm going to bed.

   ES *gets up and heads towards the stairs.* FLO *just sits. Then
   suddenly she stands up.*

FLO. And that's it, is it? End of discussion. Because you don't
    like it. As always.

   ES *turns, surprised. She's about to respond but* FLO *cuts her
   off.*

Then let me tell you what's going to happen. They will get their power of attorney and they will stick you in a nursing home. And me? There's no family coming to sweep me up. I will be out on the street. Literally. Out on the street. Because none of this is mine. My name isn't on anything. You know that, right? Of course you do. You made absolutely sure of it. Because God forbid it looks like I'm anything but the fucking lodger! God forbid anyone knows you've been having sex with a woman all this time!

And God forbid I have any fucking power in this relationship.

ES. That's enough.

FLO. Jesus! I'm the bloody idiot. Thirty-six years of doing it all your way, believing stupidly that one day you'd... Fuck!

Is that what you want, Es? For me to have nothing? After everything I've given up for you?

ES. Everything you've?! /

FLO. Because that's what it feels like. I'm doing everything I can to look after you and /

ES. I'm not a sodding invalid!

FLO. I'm following you round the house. Turning off the gas when you leave it on. Turning off taps. Pretending that you're not...

ES (*challenging her*). Not what?

Not what?

Go on...

They look at each other. This is painful for both of them.

FLO. And I'm happy to do it all. Because I choose you.

But I need you to choose me.

ES. Oh, here we go! The same old tune. How perfect for you. Now I'm a mad old woman you can get exactly what you /

FLO. That's not fair!

ES. No, *this* isn't fair! Do you think I don't know what's happening? Do you think I don't see that look in your eyes? See you watching me? Do you think I don't know I'm being babysat? Have you got any idea what that's like? How bloody frightening it is? How bloody humiliating it is?

FLO. Es, I /

ES. But I am still here. And I still get to decide what I do or don't say to my son. So yes. End of discussion.

Beat.

FLO (*quietly*). You told Kasia.

ES. What?

FLO. Kasia. You told Kasia about us. You told her all about our wedding. The bonfire, the dancing. You even taught her our fucking song!

ES (*defensively*). So?

FLO. You told a child all about us, without even thinking. And that's fine, is it? But you won't tell Peter. Even if it means losing me. Are you that ashamed of me?

A long pause where they stare at each other. Eventually FLO *gives up and goes to the sink and is trying to busy herself with washing up but is furious and upset.*

ES *watches her. She doesn't know what to do to help. She wanders to the table and sees both sets of forms and the pen. She is trying to remember what the forms are. She looks at* FLO *who still has her back to her.*

ES. Flo.

FLO. I can't, Es.

ES *wants to fix whatever is wrong. She sits and starts looking at the papers. She flicks through and then picks up the pen.* FLO *turns around.*

FLO. What are you doing?

ES. I'm supposed to sign these forms, aren't I?

> FLO *rushes over, not sure which forms she is signing.*

FLO. Which ones are you...?

ES. I'm signing the forms.

> FLO *sees that* ES *has her forms and gathers up* CATHERINE'*s slightly stealthily.*

FLO. You're signing the forms.

> *She begins signing.* FLO *is holding her breath.* ES *suddenly stops.*

ES. What are they for?

> FLO *sighs.*

FLO. They are to decide who you want to look after you.

ES. You look after me.

FLO. That's what I want.

ES. I like that.

> *They smile at each other.*

And Peter wants me to sign these forms?

> FLO *chooses her words carefully.*

FLO. Peter wants you to... Yes. Peter wants you to sign these forms too.

ES. Right. And these are Peter's forms?

FLO. They... are the... same forms Peter wants you to sign.

> ES *stares at the forms.* FLO *is struggling.*

Are you going to sign them then?

ES. Yes, right.

> ES *looks at* FLO *and then signs the forms.* FLO *flicks through to another page.*

FLO. And here.

ES. Right.

She signs.

Done?

FLO. That's your bit done.

ES. Thank you for your help.

FLO *can't answer. She just hugs* ES.

FLO. I will take good care of you.

ES. You'd better! Right. I'm shattered. I'm off to bed.

ES *gets up.*

FLO. But it's only /

ES. What?

FLO. Never mind. I'll be up in a bit.

ES *exits.* FLO *looks at the forms* ES *has signed.*

She is struggling with what to do about the forms. They end up hidden in a drawer.

Scene Three

ES *is in the kitchen. She quietly commentates on her actions to try and keep herself on track.*

ES. Tea.

Fill the kettle.

Kettle on.

Teapot.

She starts looking for the teapot.

Teapot. Teapot. Teapot.

She cannot find the teapot and instead finds two mugs by the sink and puts them next to the kettle. She looks at them, frowning until the kettle boils and she snaps back into motion.

Tea.

She smiles. She can do this. She starts looking for teabags and sees a loaf of bread. She picks up the bread and smells it.

Toast.

She takes two slices of bread and stares at them for a moment. She looks around the kitchen.

Toast.

She goes over to the oven and opens it. She turns on the grill.

Grill. Gas. Lit.

She checks it is lit. She looks around and sees the bread. She smells it again then looks back at the grill. She can't work out what to do next. She looks around. She finds a plate on the sink. She puts the bread on the plate and puts the plate under the grill.

Toast. Jam.

She wanders around the kitchen unable to work out where the jam is. It is as if she can't see the cupboards.

Jam. Jam. Jam. Jam.

She begins to get frustrated.

Oh God!

She sees the mugs. Relief.

Ah. Tea.

She turns the kettle on. She smiles. She can do this. The kettle boils.

Milk.

*She goes and gets the milk from the fridge and returns to
the mugs. She stares at the milk. It doesn't make sense. She
stands for a long time. Smoke starts to come from the grill.
She doesn't notice. She looks at the mugs, the milk still in
her hand. Eventually the smoke alarm goes off. The noise
frightens ES. She drops the milk and puts her hands over her
ears. FLO comes running down the stairs.*

FLO. What the…? Es!

FLO comes in and sees the smoking grill and the plate.

Fuck's sake!

*She turns the grill off, grabs a tea towel and starts waving it
in the air underneath the smoke alarm. ES still has her hands
over her ears.*

Es!

ES looks around slightly helplessly.

Open the back door!

ES looks around.

Es! The back door. Open it.

*FLO opens the back door. The smoke alarm stops. FLO uses
the tea towel to get the hot plate out from under the grill. She
drops it into the sink.*

What were you doing?!

ES. –

FLO. Es?!

ES. –

FLO. What were you doing? You can't /

ES. Don't shout /

FLO. You could have started a fire. What were you doing?

ES. I was hungry.

FLO. Why didn't you use the toaster?

ES. I couldn't find it.

FLO (*exasperated*). It's just there.

ES. Stop shouting at me!

> ES *storms out of the room.*

FLO. Es!

> ES *starts going up the stairs and we hear a crash.*

> Fuck! Es?

> FLO *runs to the stairs to help* ES.

> Oh God, don't move. Let me look at you.

ES. Stop fussing.

FLO. Did you slip?

ES. Ow!

FLO. You've scraped your leg. Don't get up.

ES. I'm fine.

FLO. Okay, let me /

ES. Ow.

FLO. Hold onto me. That's it. I've got you. I've got you.

> FLO *supports* ES *who is limping slightly.*

> Come on. Let's get you on the sofa. God, you're limping. Is it sore?

ES. I'm fine. Don't fuss.

FLO. I'm going to get something to clean up your leg.

> FLO *goes to the sink and gets out a first-aid box from under the sink.* ES *is uncomfortable and starts to get up.*

ES. Ooh.

> FLO *turns round and sees her.*

FLO. Stay still. I'm just getting the /

ES. My head hurts.

> FLO *comes straight over.*

FLO. Did you bang your head?

> FLO *starts looking at and feeling* ES*'s head.*

ES. What are you doing?

Ow! Stop fussing.

FLO. What happened?

ES. I don't know.

FLO. Try to remember.

ES. What?

FLO. Oh God, Es! I need to know whether you can't remember because you've got concussion or whether you just... can't remember. Shit.

ES. Concussion?

FLO. You fell down the stairs.

ES. I'm fine.

FLO. I... Okay. Let me look at your leg.

It's just a bit of a graze.

> *She wipes it and puts a plaster on.*

There you go. You're okay.

> FLO *packs up the first-aid kit and heads back to the kitchen. She turns back to watch* ES, *worried.*

I'll make you some tea.

ES. I feel a bit sick actually.

> FLO*'s mind is racing.*

FLO. Okay. Let me get you some water. Just relax. You'll be alright in a minute.

FLO *is not as sure as she is trying to sound. She is getting*
ES *a glass of water when the front door opens.* BEATA *calls*
from the door.

BEATA. Hello!

KASIA *comes running in followed by* BEATA *with several of*
KASIA*'s bags.*

KASIA. It smells like bonfires in here!

ES. Hello, cariad.

FLO. Kasia, be careful with Esmee. She's had a bit of a fall.

BEATA. Is she okay? Are you okay, Esmee?

BEATA *crosses to the sofa to look at* ES. *She looks at* FLO.

What happened?

FLO. She grazed her leg.

BEATA. Is that all?

You okay, Esmee?

ES. I'm fine.

BEATA. Does anywhere else hurt?

ES. Just a bit of a headache.

BEATA. Did you hit your head?

(*To* FLO.) Did she hit her head?

FLO *doesn't answer.*

BEATA *holds up four fingers.*

Esmee. Can you see how many fingers I'm holding up?

ES. Fifty-six!

ES *and* KASIA *giggle.*

BEATA. Esmee. How many fingers?

ES. Four.

BEATA. What happened?

ES. Nothing but trouble. That's what my husband used to say!

BEATA. You are no trouble. I'm just going to have a quick check of your head okay?

ES. Check it's still screwed on straight!

She and KASIA *laugh again.*

BEATA *feels her head and when she touches the back* ES *flinches.*

BEATA. Sorry, Esmee.

ES. I'm fine. A cup of tea would be nice.

FLO. I'm just making it.

BEATA *hands* KASIA *her phone.*

BEATA. Here, Kasia – show Esmee those funny videos you found.

BEATA *gets up and crosses to* FLO.

If she hit her head, we need to take her to hospital.

FLO. I didn't see. I was in here.

BEATA. When I touched the back of her head /

ES *and* KASIA *laugh about something.*

FLO. She's fine. Look.

BEATA. Flo.

FLO. She doesn't want to.

BEATA. Flo.

FLO. She's fine. The last thing she needs is to go to A&E and sit there for hours.

BEATA. This time of day... They'll see her quickly anyway because she's...

FLO. She's what?

BEATA. Look it's just a precaution. Better safe than sorry, right?

FLO. –

BEATA. This is my job. She is my responsibility.

FLO. She is *my* responsibility!

BEATA. Calm down.

FLO. Don't tell me to calm down in my own home.

BEATA. Listen, Flo, I understand /

BEATA goes to physically comfort FLO *who shrugs her off.*

FLO. No you don't! How could you? You think it's so simple. You think we just walk in there and get treated like everyone else. They'll think *I'm* the carer, not you. You're so fucking naive!

BEATA. Flo! I understand all of that.

She gestures to KASIA.

FLO. She fell down a few stairs. She's fine /

BEATA. She fell down the stairs?!

FLO *realises what she's said.*

Right. We need to go.

FLO. They'll call Peter!

BEATA *looks at* FLO.

This is exactly what he needs to… That'll be it.

BEATA. You can't let that /

KASIA. Mum! Mum! Esmee has gone a bit funny.

BEATA *and* FLO *rush over.* ES *is very woozy.*

FLO. Oh fuck!

BEATA. Es, Es. Can you hear me?

ES. Flo?

FLO. I'm here. You're okay.

BEATA. Es. I need you to do something for me, okay?

FLO. Just give her a minute, will you?

BEATA. Flo! Es, I need you to lift both your arms for me.

FLO clocks what this means and doesn't like it.

FLO. She's fine. Aren't you, Es? Es?

BEATA (*quite fiercely now*). Flo. You need to let her go so I can /

FLO. Don't tell me what to /

BEATA. Flo. Let her go. Esmee, I need you to lift both your arms up for me.

FLO. Give her a minute!

BEATA. She might not have a minute. Let her go.

FLO. No. She's fine!

BEATA. And what if she isn't?!

FLO. Then she dies here with me!

BEATA stares at FLO in disbelief.

FLO has frightened herself.

Silence.

BEATA. You don't mean that.

The doorbell rings.

BEATA sends KASIA to answer it.

Kasia. (*To* ES.) Esmee, lift your arms up for me.

KASIA and opens it. It's CATHERINE. *Meanwhile* FLO *and* BEATA *check that* ES *is okay. She is coming round a bit.*

CATHERINE. Oh! It's you. Is your mother here?

FLO. Oh, fuck's sake. Not now.

KASIA. Mum! It's that woman.

CATHERINE. My name is Catherine.

KASIA. It's that woman Catherine!

*CATHERINE pushes into the room with KASIA following.
KASIA runs round to be near ES. BEATA gets up to speak
to CATHERINE.*

CATHERINE. I've been sitting on that motorway for nearly
four hours and it was incredibly hot and all because you
didn't send those forms! I told you I needed them!

BEATA. Catherine, it's /

CATHERINE notices the smell of smoke.

CATHERINE. What's that smell? What's going on?

KASIA. Esmee fell down the stairs so we're taking her to the
hospital.

CATHERINE. Oh God! Are you okay, Esmee? Is she okay?

FLO. It was just a little fall.

BEATA. She hit her head.

CATHERINE. Right, well, it's a good job I was here then.
I knew something like this was going to happen.

FLO. Don't start, Catherine!

A glare from CATHERINE.

ES. Flo?

FLO. It's okay. I'm here, love. I've got you. It's okay.

*FLO is cradling ES and kisses her on the head.
CATHERINE sees this and it stops in her tracks.*

I've got you, love.

CATHERINE. Oh!

*Beat. FLO looks up and sees CATHERINE looking. She
stares back, defiant.*

Beat.

I didn't... Right.

ES. I don't feel very well.

BEATA. It's alright. We're going to take you to the hospital.

FLO looks at BEATA.

FLO. I'll drive.

CATHERINE. We can go in my car. It's a seven-seater.

BEATA. Great. Come on, Es, let's get you up.

As they start to get her up ES collapses. BEATA and FLO catch her.

FLO. Fuck! Es?

ES vomits.

ES. Sorry.

BEATA. Kasia, my bag! Don't worry Esmee. You're okay.

FLO and BEATA are virtually carrying ES.

KASIA grabs BEATA's bag and runs to get the front door.

CATHERINE nearly steps in the sick.

CATHERINE. Actually, maybe she'd be better in your car? I'll follow.

FLO throws her a look.

FLO. Shit, the back door's open.

BEATA. Come on, Es, we've got you.

BEATA and CATHERINE take ES out the door.

FLO. I'll meet you in the lane.

FLO stands for a second, overwhelmed. She goes to the kitchen and goes out the back door, locking it from the outside.

The scene ends and there is a transition sequence – the world turns upside down. A hospital waiting area and a hospital room appear.

Scene Four

In the dark a hospital room with ES *in bed.* BEATA *and* FLO *are in there with her.*

Lights up on a hospital corridor. KASIA *is sat and* CATHERINE *is standing. She is making a call.* KASIA *is watching her.*

CATHERINE. Peter, it's me again. Can you give me a call when you get this? Okay. Bye.

She hangs up.

Shit!

She sees KASIA *watching her.*

Sorry! That was a bad word. I'm just worried that Peter might... I don't want him to think I've... He just gets cross if...

KASIA. My mum says you should just ignore bullies.

CATHERINE. What?! Why would you say that? That's quite rude actually. He's not a /

KASIA *looks down at the floor a bit scared.* CATHERINE *stops herself.*

His mother is very ill and he should know.

Pause.

He's not...

Silence.

KASIA. Is Esmee going to die?

CATHERINE. Oh, gosh. I hope not. We'll have to wait and see what the doctors say.

Pause.

KASIA *looks very small and vulnerable. There are a few silent tears.*

CATHERINE *is not good with children and does not know what to do.*

CATHERINE *checks her phone again. Nothing. She searches for something to say.*

The thing is, Esmee is an old lady.

This was not useful.

She comes and sits cautiously next to KASIA.

Do you have grandparents?

KASIA. They live in Poland.

CATHERINE. Do you get to see them much?

KASIA. No.

CATHERINE. Oh, that's a shame. Do you speak to them on the phone? On Zoom?

KASIA. Mum says they won't understand me. My Polish isn't very good.

CATHERINE. But you could say hello. Couldn't your mum translate for you?

KASIA *is thinking about this. Why hasn't she ever done that?*

KASIA. Mum gets upset when she speaks to them. She doesn't like me to see her crying so I have to go to my room.

CATHERINE. Haven't you ever spoken to them?

KASIA. No.

CATHERINE *senses there is something strange.* KASIA *watches* CATHERINE's *face.*

But I've saved up and I am going to surprise Mum.

CATHERINE. Surprise her?

KASIA. I've saved up eighty pounds to buy two tickets to Poland.

CATHERINE. Eighty pounds?

KASIA. Yep. Ryan Air.

CATHERINE. But if that's all it costs then why haven't you gone before? Eighty pounds is nothing really.

KASIA thinks about this for a moment. Is this true?

KASIA. Mum can't do a full-time job because she has to look after me. So we don't have money for many treats.

CATHERINE (*beat*). Right.

Pause.

KASIA. We get treats at Flo and Es's sometimes though. Pizza, fish and chips. And Es always has Jelly Babies.

KASIA smiles and then remembers about ES.

I hope she is going to be okay.

CATHERINE. Yes. Me too.

Beat.

I think it's lovely that you've saved up, Kasia. You might want to give your mum some time to sort it all out though, when you tell her. It might be... a bit complicated.

KASIA looks at CATHERINE, who doesn't look back at her. That was an odd thing to say.

BEATA and FLO enter. FLO is tired.

How is she?

BEATA looks to FLO to answer but she doesn't. She nervously looks at FLO as she explains.

BEATA. She's sleeping. They think the fall might have caused a bleed on the brain which then caused the mini stroke. She needs to stay in for a few days at least. They'll know more when she wakes up.

CATHERINE. Okay.

BEATA. Flo. Sit down. You're exhausted.

FLO sits on a chair. KASIA goes and gives her a hug.

Why don't I go get some coffees? Maybe something to eat.

KASIA. I'm starving.

BEATA. I'm sorry, Kasia, of course. Flo?

CATHERINE *grabs her purse.*

FLO. I should go and sit with her.

BEATA. She's sleeping. Take half an hour. Please.

FLO *is too tired to fight.*

Come on, Kasia.

BEATA *and* KASIA *head off.* CATHERINE *hands* BEATA *money which she takes slightly reluctantly.* CATHERINE *stands awkwardly for a moment.* FLO *has her eyes shut.* CATHERINE *sits next to her.*

Long pause.

Eventually FLO *opens her eyes.*

CATHERINE. I wish you'd told us sooner, Flo.

FLO. Told you what?

CATHERINE. I'm not blaming you.

FLO. But you are.

CATHERINE. We didn't know things had got so bad.

FLO. And why was that?

Beat.

Nothing. All through the pandemic. No calls, nothing. And then suddenly…

Pause. This is news to CATHERINE.

CATHERINE. But he said he had.

Beat.

It was a really difficult time. His business /

FLO. Right.

CATHERINE. It's not an excuse, I know. If I'd known he hadn't been. *I* would have…

CATHERINE *stops herself.*

Look. We are where we are now and we all have to work together.

CATHERINE *looks at* FLO *who has closed her eyes again.*

Work out what happens next.

Beat.

She clearly can't stay where she is.

Beat.

Stairs are obviously a problem. The apartments we found would be perfect. Still some independence but the security of knowing there are people on hand if she needs anything.

Pause.

You can't be expected to manage all by yourself.

FLO. We're doing fine.

CATHERINE. No offence, Flo, but…

She gestures to where they are.

We can't risk another fall.

FLO. We?

CATHERINE. Yes. Look, whatever you think about us, we are her family. She's our responsibility.

FLO *takes a breath.*

And I get it, I do. I can't say I understand why you didn't tell us. It's 2023, for goodness' sake, and we're hardly monsters. But the thing is… Whatever… 'arrangement' you two have…

FLO *bristles.*

…legally it's going to fall to us to sort everything out. The house… care…

Beat.

If only we'd got those forms signed.

FLO *looks at* CATHERINE *but this is as much about her own papers as it is* CATHERINE's.

FLO. There's a lot more to it than just getting her to sign.

CATHERINE. Has she made a will?

FLO. Fucking hell, Catherine!

CATHERINE. I didn't mean /

FLO. Didn't you?

CATHERINE. Look, you can be angry with me as much as you like, but someone here needs to think about the practicalities of looking after Esmee. We are spending a small fortune sending Beata in three times a week and that won't be enough after this. What if she can't wash herself or feed herself or...?

FLO. Jesus!

Pause.

CATHERINE. I'm thinking of you here too, Flo. You don't have to do this on your own.

FLO. Don't /

CATHERINE. She'd be better off in a flat. She'd be happier if she could see Peter more often. Beata says she talks about him a lot. It would give them a chance to reconnect before it's too late.

FLO. And what am I supposed to do?

Beat. CATHERINE *has an idea.*

CATHERINE. Perhaps we could get you a double apartment? I'd have to talk to Peter obviously but yes, that would be the thing! I can phone the place later and see what they've got available. That's perfect! It'll be just like here but closer to us and with that extra support. You two can come and visit for Sunday lunch. It will be lovely.

FLO *doesn't respond.* CATHERINE *is thinking this through.*

She is delighted with her idea.

Of course, it will be a bit more expensive, but I'm sure we can work something out. We'll be family.

FLO. Family?

CATHERINE. Yes!

FLO *reacts*.

What?

FLO. One visit a year, if she was lucky, for years. And now, all of a sudden, you want to play happy families? And you expect me to believe this has nothing to do with getting hold of the house and money and /

CATHERINE. That's not /

FLO. Isn't it?

CATHERINE *is hurt and lashes out*.

CATHERINE. She fell down the stairs.

FLO. It was an accident.

CATHERINE. Where were you?

FLO. What?

CATHERINE. You should have been watching her.

FLO *is about to respond when* BEATA *and* KASIA *return*.

KASIA. We got Jelly Babies for Es!

BEATA *notices the tension. She hands them coffees*.

BEATA. Everything okay?

CATHERINE. Yes fine.

Beat.

I was just saying to Flo that perhaps we can get her and Esmee a double apartment in the scheme we found. I think it would be perfect. The best of everything for Esmee. Don't you think, Beata?

BEATA *looks at* FLO *questioningly.*

BEATA. Well, I…

FLO *snaps.*

FLO. You could try asking Es?! Instead of acting like she's /

CATHERINE. Fine. I will.

CATHERINE *starts to head off.*

FLO. Catherine!

CATHERINE *has gone.*

Shit.

FLO *goes to go after her.*

BEATA. Leave her. Es is sleeping anyway.

It'll be fine.

FLO *sighs and collapses in the chair.*

BEATA *offers* FLO *a sandwich.*

Flo.

FLO. I'm not hungry.

KASIA. You can have a bit of mine if you like.

FLO *smiles at* KASIA.

FLO. Thank you, sweetheart.

BEATA. It's going to be okay.

The lights fade on the corridor and come up on ES's *room.*

Scene Five

ES *is sat up in bed.* CATHERINE *enters.* ES *struggles slightly for thoughts and words and possibly slurs slightly. It improves gradually throughout the scene.*

ES. Flo?

> CATHERINE *crosses to the bed.*

CATHERINE. Hello, Esmee. It's Catherine. How are you feeling?

ES. I'm fine. A bit… sore head.

CATHERINE. Well, you fell down the stairs.

ES. My… fault.

CATHERINE. You need to be careful, Esmee.

ES. Sorry.

> *Pause.*

> Anyone else…?

CATHERINE. They are all outside. I wanted to see you by myself.

ES. Peter?

CATHERINE. He's not here. I've tried /

ES. Good… My little boy.

CATHERINE. Hardly a boy any more.

ES. No. Little man, all… grown up.

> CATHERINE *is struck by this.* ES *gestures for* CATHERINE *to sit next to her bed. She glances towards the door and speaks conspiratorially.*

> I need you to… talk… to Peter

CATHERINE. Okay.

ES. About where I'm going to... Home.

CATHERINE. Right.

CATHERINE *is expecting a fight.*

ES *takes* CATHERINE*'s hands and looks very intently at her.*

ES. I can't go home.

CATHERINE *is surprised.*

CATHERINE. Okay.

ES. It's not... good for me there.

CATHERINE. No, I don't think you are being looked after well enough.

ES. That's... not fair. My fault. Nothing but trouble. I... get things wrong. It's... It's... better if...

CATHERINE. Now, Esmee. You can't help it.

ES. Better if I... stay somewhere else.

CATHERINE. It's all being arranged.

ES *smiles at her a little sadly.*

ES. Tell him I love him... very much?

CATHERINE. –

ES. When I'm better I'll...

There is a hint of tears which she is doing a good job of holding back.

Jim... /

CATHERINE. Esmee, you /

ES. I wasn't what he... expected... as a wife.

CATHERINE. Esmee?

ES. I haven't... been easy for him.

But I... I can't go back.

CATHERINE. –

ES. He will take care of Peter, won't he? Just till I can…

CATHERINE. Esmee? Are you okay? Do you know where you are?

ES looks around her.

ES. I fell. It was my fault.

CATHERINE. Do you remember what happened?

ES. It was silly. I was… I was… the top of the stairs and…

She is remembering. It is difficult.

CATHERINE. Yes…

She looks at the door.

ES. He loses his temper. I should know better…

Beat.

CATHERINE. Jim?

ES. He didn't know about… the baby.

Long pause. CATHERINE understands. They look at each other. CATHERINE takes ES's hand. They both sit in silence for a moment thinking about their own losses.

CATHERINE. Oh, Esmee. I know how hard that is.

ES. Peter will need some help.

CATHERINE. He's going to need his mum.

ES. He'll be okay. No silly Mum to… Tell him be a good boy. Tidy room, piano practice, help his dad.

CATHERINE. It's not the same.

ES. Jim won't…

CATHERINE. What?

ES. He'll be better when I'm not there.

ES *is toughening up.*

CATHERINE *is piecing things together.*

A long pause.

CATHERINE. Why didn't you go back for him?

ES *works hard to find the right word.*

ES. Unfit.

Pause.

Maybe it was better. They're the same. Peas in a pod.

This hurts.

Long pause. Neither of them are looking at each other.

ES *suddenly turns and notices* CATHERINE.

Do you work here?

CATHERINE *is broken out of her moment.*

Where's Flo?

CATHERINE *realises it has ended.*

CATHERINE. She's outside.

ES. She'll be worried.

CATHERINE. She's fine.

ES. I get a bit lost without her.

CATHERINE. –

ES. Can you get her?

CATHERINE. –

ES. I need Flo.

CATHERINE *gets up and starts moving towards the door.
Before she reaches it she turns back.*

CATHERINE. Esmee?

ES looks up.

He needed you.

They look at each other for a long while.

ES. I need Flo.

CATHERINE *nods and leaves the room.*

CATHERINE *leans on the wall outside the room. Thoughts and feelings swimming. Her mobile rings. She takes it out and looks at it. It is Peter.*

CATHERINE *pulls herself together and answers the call.*

CATHERINE. Peter.

The lights fade on CATHERINE.

Scene Six

Lights back up on the hospital corridor. BEATA *and* FLO *sit next to each other.* KASIA *is sat on the floor leaning on a chair doing some drawing.*

FLO. I should have brought her straight here. What was I thinking?

BEATA. You were scared.

FLO. I don't know what I'd do. / She's all I've got.

KASIA. You've got us.

FLO. Thank you, sweetheart.

KASIA. Mum, when Esmee wakes up, can I read her some of my new book?

BEATA. Kasia, I /

FLO. I think she'd love that. You know that's what she used to do at Greenham? Read books with the children.

KASIA. There were children at Greenham?

FLO. Yeah. Especially in the holidays.

KASIA. Cool!

FLO. Every week. Rain or shine. She'd turn up with her flask of tea, a bag of books and a packet of jammie dodgers. They called her the biscuit lady.

KASIA *laughs*.

I would volunteer to help her. And we'd talk… about everything…

I was young and had a lot of opinions but she never made me feel stupid.

BEATA. She's kind.

FLO. Yeah. And clever. And…

KASIA. Funny.

FLO. Yes. And infuriating. But [everything]…

I know you think we've missed out on stuff because /

BEATA. Flo, I don't /

FLO. When she looks at me. It's like I'm the only person in the world.

And that's enough. Even on the difficult days.

There was this time at her school. I was delivering cakes for Red Nose Day. Being the 'helpful housemate'. And the staff and parents were all telling me how wonderful she was. And I wanted to scream at them 'I know. I know her better than all of you.'

And then she looked at me across the playground. And there it was. Everything. All fine. Just us.

And that's still there, you know. Some days she's her old self. Right? And I wonder if I'm imagining it all. /

BEATA. / Flo. You're / [not]

FLO. I know. I know I'm not but... How is that? How is it that one day... one minute even... she can be fine, dancing round the kitchen with me and then the next, she's looking at me like she has no idea where she is? How is that possible?

BEATA. That's just how it is.

FLO. It's cruel.

BEATA *nods*.

And it's lonely.

BEATA. Is there no one in your family that you...?

FLO *shakes her head*.

You've been amazing. Managing all this.

FLO. She'd have been so much better at it than me.

BEATA. You just need to talk to each other.

FLO. She won't. If she doesn't like a conversation she... She won't do confrontation. And I can't make her.

Years ago. We were arguing about something and I raised my voice. And for a second, there was this look in her eyes. Like she was frightened of me.

I just couldn't...

That was the life that she'd left behind. I...

BEATA. You are not Jim.

FLO. But that's the look she gets now. Frightened. I can't bear it.

BEATA. That's not you, that's the dementia.

This is new. And big.

FLO. I had one job. To make her feel safe. And...

She gestures at where they are.

BEATA. Look. She won't always feel safe. It's hard and confusing. But you can make sure that she *is* safe.

And you'll get help. Us... more if you need it.

FLO. I don't know. Maybe Catherine is right. Maybe /

CATHERINE *comes back in. She is slightly shell-shocked.*

BEATA. Catherine? Are you okay?

FLO. Is there something wrong with Es?

CATHERINE. I spoke to Peter.

FLO. And?

CATHERINE. He already knew. About the two of you. That you're... He just laughed at me when I told him.

Pause.

BEATA. Does he still want to move her?

KASIA *starts to listen.*

CATHERINE. Yep.

FLO *is thinking.*

FLO. So we move, I guess.

Beat. CATHERINE *has more.*

CATHERINE. Sorry, Flo. He won't. She moves on her own, or it's nothing. No Beata, no help. nothing.

BEATA *and* FLO *are shocked.* KASIA *is furious.*

BEATA. But that's...

Then we manage by ourselves. The doctor's said she'll probably make a good recovery.

CATHERINE. She just talked to me for ten minutes thinking it was forty years ago.

FLO. She's awake?

BEATA. We'll go and check on her. Kasia.

KASIA *glares at* CATHERINE *as she gathers up her things. Just as she is about to go.*

KASIA. They have to be together. Es wouldn't want to move without Flo.

Everyone looks at KASIA.

BEATA. Come on Kasia.

She turns and follows BEATA *to* ES*'s room.*

Silence.

CATHERINE. I'm sorry.

Pause.

FLO. All this time. He knew. Seems like everybody did.

CATHERINE. Not me. Peter's right. I'm a 'Stupid –

FLO. Little Woman'.

CATHERINE. ?

FLO. Jim.

CATHERINE. Oh.

Silence.

BEATA *runs in.*

BEATA. You need to come!

FLO leaps out of her seat and runs. BEATA *follows.* CATHERINE *pauses for a moment. Her world is upside down. Then she follows them.*

The scene ends and there is a transition. Sounds of Greenham mixed with hospital sounds and movement inside and around ES*'s room. It eventually settles into quiet stillness.*

Scene Seven

ES's hospital room. ES is asleep, propped up. FLO is in a chair next to the bed and has fallen asleep onto the bed. KASIA and BEATA are asleep on a chair. CATHERINE is sat facing downstage reading the assisted living brochure. Her phone lights up with a call. She looks and cancels it. A few moments later it lights up again with a message. She doesn't read it.

ES comes to.

ES. Flo?

FLO wakes up. CATHERINE stays very still, listening.

FLO. Es.

ES. Where am I?

FLO. You're in the hospital. It's okay.

It's okay. How do you feel?

ES is looking at the hospital gown she is in. She runs her hand along it.

ES. Horrible.

This makes FLO laugh and then she is crying. Relieved. ES looks at her and touches her face.

FLO. I'm okay.

ES. You're... Tears.

FLO. I'm fine.

ES. Where am I?

FLO. You're in the hospital.

ES. Am I ill?.

FLO. You've had a couple of little strokes. You fell. Do you remember?

ES shakes her head.

You scared me.

ES. Sorry.

FLO. Don't be silly. *I'm* sorry.

ES. Why?

FLO. I…

She is trying not to cry.

ES *looks around. She sees* BEATA *and* KASIA.

ES. Who…?

FLO. Beata and Kasia. Catherine is here too. No one wanted to leave. We've set up camp.

Silence.

ES. Where am I?

FLO. We're in the hospital. You had a fall.

ES. I'm sorry.

FLO. It's okay.

FLO *kisses* ES*'s hand.*

Pause.

ES. Am I ill?

FLO. You should try and get some sleep. It's very late.

ES. You… coming to bed?

FLO. I'm okay here. You try and sleep.

It's quiet for a bit but ES *is awake.*

ES. Flo, can we go home?

FLO. We can't, love, it's late. And the doctors need to keep an eye on you.

ES. I'm fine.

FLO. I know but…

ES. I want to… go home.

FLO. I know.

ES starts trying to get up. FLO *doesn't know how to stop her. She points at* BEATA *and* KASIA.

Es. The little one is sleeping. You don't want to wake her do you?

ES. Oh. No. Stay quiet.

FLO. Good idea.

FLO tucks her back in a bit.

You comfy?

ES. Comfy?

FLO. Try and close your eyes for a bit.

ES. Thank you.

Pause.

I fell?

FLO. Yes, love.

ES. I can't go back.

FLO is surprised.

FLO. Well. Peter has found somewhere very nice.

ES. Peter.

FLO. Yes, near him. So you could see him more often. Would you like that?

ES. Yes.

FLO. Do you want to move?

ES. With you?

FLO. I could visit.

ES. I want to stay with you.

FLO. I don't know if… I don't know if I can look after you, Es.

ES. You always look after me.

FLO. –

> CATHERINE's *phone lights up again and she cancels the call.*

ES. I'm forgetting a lot, aren't I?

FLO. –

ES. Is it worse now?

FLO. The doctors don't know.

> *Pause.*

ES. You shouldn't have to... be my nurse.

FLO. I... You scared me today. If Beata hadn't been there I...

ES. I'm sorry.

FLO. Es.

ES. Nothing but trouble.

FLO. Please don't say that. That's not what I meant. I'm not Jim. I choose you.

> *They look at each other.*

ES. I choose you.

> *This lands.*

> *Pause.*

> I want to go home.

FLO. I know. The thing is, Peter /

ES. I should talk to Peter.

> *Beat.*

FLO. He knows.

ES. Oh.

> ES *takes this in.*

FLO. I'm sorry. I know you didn't…

Pause.

ES. I was ashamed.

Beat. This hurts FLO.

Of myself, never of you. Never of you.

Possibly the most honest moment they have ever shared.

I've been a bit of a shit, haven't I?

FLO. Not every day.

A quiet laugh from them both.

ES. Can we go home?

FLO. Not tonight. You need to rest. Close your eyes. Try and get some sleep.

ES. Will you stay with me?

FLO. Always.

ES. I…

FLO. I know.

They hold hands. ES eventually closes her eyes and starts to fall asleep. FLO watches her. FLO's world is upside down. Eventually she closes her eyes too.

Silence.

CATHERINE's phone lights up again. She eventually answers it, slightly defiantly.

CATHERINE. Peter. Now's not a good time.

She hangs up.

The scene ends and there is a transition – a sense of restoration and a return to the domestic as the hospital disappears back into the house. There are a few disruptions that remain, scars of what has occurred.

Scene Eight

ES *and* FLO*'s house. We hear the door open and* KASIA *comes in first followed by* BEATA.

She spots the vomit on the floor.

KASIA. Urrggh. Mum! Es's sick is still /

BEATA. It's fine. I'll clear it up. Where's your banner?

KASIA. In my bag.

BEATA. Get it ready then. They'll be here soon.

> BEATA *goes to the kitchen and fills the kettle.* KASIA *gets a homemade banner out of her bag. She unfolds it. It reads 'WELCOME HOME ES'.*

KASIA. Mum. I'm glad you came to work here.

> BEATA *smiles.*

BEATA. Why?

KASIA. Because otherwise we wouldn't have met Es and Flo.

BEATA. That's true.

> *Pause.*

> KASIA *is working out where to put the banner.*

> *The front door opens.* FLO *and* ES *come in.*

FLO. Here we are.

> *She sees* KASIA.

> Hello.

KASIA. Welcome home!

> *She holds up her banner.*

ES. Oh lovely! Did you make that?

KASIA. Yes!

BEATA. Hi Es.

BEATA *comes over.* ES *nearly steps in the vomit.*

Careful.

FLO. Oh! I, I've hardly been here. I just didn't get a chance to /

BEATA. It's fine.

ES *stops as she notices she has her coat on.*

ES. Are we going somewhere? Why have we got our coats on?

KASIA (*laughing*). You just got in.

ES. Silly old me.

BEATA. Es, you should probably get into bed. Flo will take you up.

ES. Is it late?

BEATA. Not so late. But you need to rest a bit.

FLO. I'll take you up and get you tucked in, shall I?

BEATA. We'll see you tomorrow, Esmee. It's good to have you home.

KASIA. Nos da.

ES. Nos da, sweetheart.

FLO *takes* ES *upstairs.*

Lovely banner.

BEATA *fills a bowl with water from the kettle and starts cleaning up the vomit.*

Pause.

KASIA. Mum?

BEATA. Yes.

KASIA. I was thinking…

BEATA. Yes…?

KASIA. Well, I've been saving up and I was going to see if we could go to Poland.

Beat. BEATA *freezes.*

BEATA. Kasia. We need to talk about that /

KASIA. But… I was thinking maybe we could go camping with Flo and Es instead. When Es is feeling a bit better. It would be like Greenham.

Pause. BEATA *just looks at* KASIA. KASIA *turns around when there is no response.*

What do you think?

BEATA. I think that is a lovely idea, Kasia.

KASIA *smiles.*

Es might not be able to manage camping though.

KASIA (*disappointed*). Oh.

BEATA. We could maybe go for a picnic or something like that?

KASIA. Okay.

Pause.

BEATA *finishes cleaning but stays on her knees for a moment.*

KASIA *turns again and beams at* BEATA.

FLO *re-enters. she sees* BEATA *on the floor.*

FLO. You shouldn't have /

BEATA *takes the water back to the sink and rinses the bowl.*

BEATA. It's what I am here for. Kasia, it's time to go.

FLO. A cup of tea?

FLO *looks at* BEATA *hopefully.*

BEATA. A very quick one. I have to get Kasia home to bed. School tomorrow.

KASIA. Boring!

FLO fills the teapot. BEATA gets headphones out of her bag and gives her phone to KASIA.

BEATA. You can have five minutes on this okay?

KASIA. Yes!

FLO. Shit.

FLO realises she has no milk. BEATA pulls some out of her bag and smiles. They sit at the table and BEATA pours them both a tea. FLO is staring slightly into the distance.

KASIA checks that FLO and BEATA aren't looking. She pulls the twenty-pound note out of her pocket and slips it back into the ornament. She checks they haven't noticed, smiles and settles herself on the sofa.

BEATA. You okay?

It breaks FLO's moment.

FLO. What? Oh, yes.

BEATA. Glad to be home?

FLO. I wasn't sure we'd get back here.

BEATA. It's good.

Pause.

FLO. I'm losing her.

BEATA. We don't know what Peter…

FLO. That's not [what I meant]…

BEATA. Oh.

FLO. How long do you think?

BEATA. Everyone is different. Es is relatively young and fairly healthy. Maybe years.

FLO nods.

One day at a time.

FLO *gets up and goes to the drawer where she put the LPA forms. She brings them to the table.* BEATA *thinks they are Catherine's forms.*

Flo, you don't need to do that. You can /

She reads the front page.

Oh. These are for *you* to /

She flicks through.

And she signed them.

FLO. There was no witness though.

BEATA *is still looking through.*

Is it too late?

BEATA. What? No. Es is still… It's not too late.

FLO. Peter?

BEATA. Let's look at them tomorrow and make a plan.

Beat.

This is good, Flo.

Pause. BEATA *looks over at* KASIA. *It's time to go.* FLO *senses it.*

FLO. You should get going.

BEATA. I'm sorry. Will you be okay?

FLO. Yeah.

Beat. They both drink their tea.

Thank you, Beata.

BEATA. And thank you, Flo.

FLO. What for?

BEATA. Kasia adores you.

FLO. You are very lucky to have her.

BEATA. We are very lucky to have you. Really.

They smile at each other.

BEATA *looks at the time. She knocks back her tea.*

Right. We'll be back tomorrow. Kasia. Come and say goodbye to Flo.

KASIA *comes to the kitchen and gives* FLO *a hug.* BEATA *collects their things.*

They are saying goodbye and BEATA *hugs* FLO. *It is the first time. A little awkward but possibly the beginning of something new.*

FLO. I'll see you both tomorrow.

KASIA. Nos da.

FLO *hugs* KASIA.

FLO. Nos da, cariad.

FLO *shows them out.*

BEATA. Pa pa.

FLO. Bye.

FLO *looks around.*

ES *has come down the stairs. She is in her nightdress.*

What are you doing up?

ES. I've lost my glasses.

FLO. They are upstairs by the bed.

ES. What would I do without you?

ES *takes* FLO's *face in her hands and kisses her.* ES *goes back to bed.*

The house is still. It is getting dark outside.

FLO *gets a bottle of wine, a glass and her pouch of tobacco.*

She sits at the table and pours herself a glass.

She rolls herself a cigarette.

She is about to get up to go and smoke outside and stops. She sits and is about to light the cigarette when the doorbell rings. FLO *goes to the door. It's* CATHERINE.

FLO. Catherine.

CATHERINE. I'm sorry, I know it's late. Can I?

FLO. Yes.

CATHERINE *enters with an overnight bag.* FLO *is anxious. The two women look at each other.* CATHERINE *opens her bag and pulls out some milk.*

CATHERINE. I thought you might need some milk.

Beat. FLO *looks at her bag.*

And some help?

FLO. Has Peter…?

CATHERINE. He shouldn't get his way this time.

FLO. Oh. Are you okay?

CATHERINE *proffers the milk.*

CATHERINE. Tea?

FLO *makes the decision to trust her.*

FLO: How about a glass of wine?

CATHERINE *laughs a laugh on the edge of tears.*

CATHERINE: Yes please.

FLO *gets her a glass. They sit.* FLO *pours* CATHERINE *some wine.*

Blackout.

TEDDY BEARS' PICNIC

On 1st April 1983, two hundred women broke into the Greenham Common airbase dressed as teddy bears and Easter bunnies to have a picnic. The following is an imagined meeting of a young Es and Flo on that day. A first date and the start of their love story.

Greenham Common 1983. FLO, *a Black woman in her early twenties, is dressed as a teddy bear and is holding a full bin bag. Behind her is a fence and on the floor a ladder. She is looking around.*

FLO. For fuck's sake!

ES, a white schoolteacher in her early thirties, enters. Woolly hat, scarf and wellies. She is carrying a flask. She laughs when she sees FLO.

ES. Perfect!

FLO. You want to come?

ES. Oh no! I was just making some tea.

FLO. Go on. I've got a spare bear suit and Maggie hasn't shown up. I can't lug it all the way over.

ES....

FLO. Go on! It's going to be fun. And you can bring the tea. It is a picnic after all.

ES. I couldn't.

FLO. I promise not to bite.

ES laughs.

FLO pulls down the hood of the bear suit and growls at ES.

Flo.

ES. I know.

FLO looks at ES *expectantly.*

Oh, sorry. I'm Es. Esmee.

FLO. Nice to meet you, Es. Now come on. Come for a picnic with me.

ES. Really, I…

FLO. What?

ES. I… I could take the costume back for you. If it's too much to carry.

FLO. You could. Or you could dress up as a bear, climb over this fence with me and we can have our first date over there with your tea and my digestives.

ES *smiles, embarrassed.*

I've brought a blanket. It's only small but I'm sure we can cuddle up.

FLO *is enjoying playing with* ES.

Seriously, look at me. Hot right?

They both laugh.

Come on, Es. For me? I can't do it on my own. We'll be a team.

ES.…

FLO *opens the bag and pulls out a bear suit.*

FLO. I think you'd make a pretty cute bear.

ES *starts to realise she is being flirted with.*

Come on.

ES. I…

FLO. For me?

FLO *holds out the legs.*

Just step in.

ES *gives in.* FLO *pulls the suit up and is now standing face to face with* ES *very close. They smile at each other and there is a flicker of a moment.*

Right, arms in.

ES *is slightly mesmerised by* FLO *and puts her arms into the suit.*

Nearly there. You look adorable.

FLO *does up the suit at the back and comes to stand back in front of her.*

Well, I'm bloody glad Maggie didn't show now. I am going in with the most beautiful bear at the picnic.

ES....

FLO. Alright then?

ES....

FLO. You've got it on now.

ES *surrenders.*

ES. Alright then.

FLO. Yes!! Right. I'll hold the ladder and then I can pass you the bag when you're up the top.

ES. How do we get down the other side?

FLO. Jump.

ES. Oh god!

FLO. You'll be fine. Soft landing.

ES. What?

FLO. All that fur.

ES. Oh yes.

FLO. Here we go then.

FLO *gets the ladder and leans it against the fence. She helps* ES *up. At the top* ES *nervously climbs onto a slanted section of barbed wire at the top of the fence.* FLO *hands her up the bag.*

Throw it down and then jump.

ES. I'm not sure…

FLO. I tell you what. I'll come up and we'll jump together. Okay?

ES. Sorry. Thanks.

FLO. No problem. Always happy to help a beautiful lady.

ES *laughs*. FLO *climbs up and onto the slanted section*.

Right. Throw that bag down.

ES *drops the bag*.

Now, on three. One. Two. Three.

ES. I…

FLO *laughs*.

FLO. I tell you what. I'll jump down then I can catch you, okay?

ES. How will we get back later?

FLO. My guess is we won't be going back that way.

ES. Why? Oh. I see.

FLO *jumps*.

Oh!

FLO. Come on. I'll catch you.

ES. Okay.

ES *jumps and* FLO *catches her. They land on the floor together.* ES *laughs nervously.*

FLO. See, that wasn't so bad, was it?

ES. Thank you.

FLO. You're welcome.

FLO *plants a kiss on* ES*'s forehead*.

Right. One more thing before we take our seats.

ES. What?

FLO *rummages in the bin bag and pulls out a jar of honey.*

FLO. You are plenty sweet enough already but…

FLO *opens the jar and scoops out some honey.*

Arms up.

ES. What?

FLO. Arms up

ES. What are you…

FLO *lifts her own arm and smears the honey over the armpit of her bear suit.*

FLO. For when they pick us up. Sticky hands.

ES. Oh. I see. That's clever.

FLO *does her other armpit and then takes another scoop.*

FLO. Come on then.

ES *raises her arms and lets* FLO *put honey on her armpits. They are very close to each other again.*

Pretty good so far, right? As first dates go.

ES. I'm not…

FLO. Shhh… Don't crush a girl's dreams just yet, eh? At Greenham you can be whatever you want. Even two teddy bears going on a romantic picnic together.

ES *looks at* FLO *who is grinning at her.* ES *can't help but smile back.*

ES. Okay then.

They smile at each other.

FLO. Right. Let's find the others and crack into that tea of yours.

FLO *sneaks a kiss on* ES*'s cheek and takes her by the hand.*

ES. Oh.

ES *looks at their hands and back up at* FLO.

We hear police voices off.

POLICE. Come away from there!

FLO *lets go of* ES*'s hand.*

FLO. Shit!

ES *grabs* FLO*'s hand back and pulls her to the ground. They both lay down on their backs, laughing.*

Blackout.

A Nick Hern Book

Es & Flo first published in Great Britain as a paperback original in 2023 by Nick Hern Books Limited, The Glasshouse, 49a Goldhawk Road, London W12 8QP, in association with Wales Millennium Centre

Es & Flo copyright © 2023 Jennifer Lunn
Teddy Bears' Picnic copyright © 2023 Jennifer Lunn

Jennifer Lunn has asserted her right to be identified as the author of this work

Cover artwork by Wales Millennium Centre with photography by Kirsten McTernan

Designed and typeset by Nick Hern Books, London
Printed in Great Britain by Mimeo Ltd, Huntingdon, Cambridgeshire PE29 6XX

A CIP catalogue record for this book is available from the British Library

ISBN 9781 83904 140 2

Woodland
CARBON
www.woodlandcarbon.co.uk
NICK HERN BOOKS
Printed on Carbon Captured paper

www.nickhernbooks.co.uk

facebook.com/nickhernbooks

twitter.com/nickhernbooks